The Life of Riley

Living with Duchenne Muscular Dystrophy, Through a Mother's Eyes

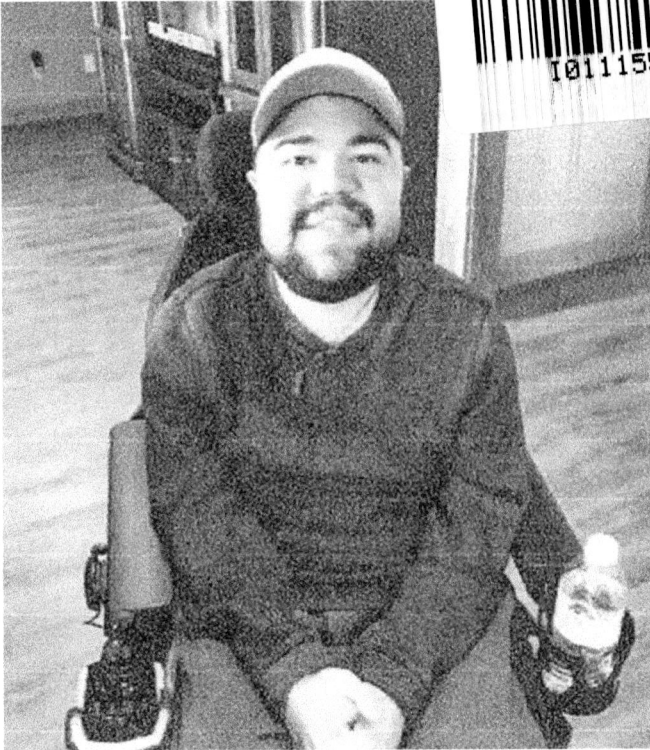

By

Dianne DeMille, Ph.D. & Nina Stuart Herrera

Born in 1969 in Butte, Montana, the author was the youngest of five children in a close family, including two brothers who were diagnosed with Spinal muscular atrophy (SMA), which is caused by recessive genes (muscular dystrophy is the umbrella term for a variety of neuromuscular diseases). When her son, Riley, was diagnosed with Duchenne muscular dystrophy (DMD) at age 4 [3] in 1995, Herrera drew on her parents' example to seek the best treatments, advocate for his rights, and still maintain "a safe, happy, nurtured, and respected environment for our family." Unlike SMA, Riley's DMD was caused by a spontaneous genetic mutation. The prognosis was dire; the author was initially told he would be dead by age 17. Tirelessly searching for experts and support, Herrera and her husband Ron connected with Parent Project Muscular Dystrophy (PPMD), an organization devoted to research and support for families affected by DMD. At age 14, Riley's heart (which is a muscle) was attacked by "The Beast," their nickname for DMD. Cincinnati Children's Hospital accepted him for a heart transplant, which he received on March 30 [31[, 2007. Riley exceeded all expectations, graduating high school and college and living fully until DMD claimed his life at age 31. Herrera vividly portrays a remarkable young man who powered through difficult times with "resilience, optimism, grace and dignity, strength and fortitude." Her own recollections, combined with reflections of others involved in Riley's life, effectively describe how fraught negotiating the evolving research and care protocols is, along with the importance and difficulty of keeping some level of normalcy in family life. The insights of the author's brothers, especially about their experiences with SMA and their close connection with Riley, add depth and a multigenerational aspect to the memoir. While emphasizing the power of positivity, Herrera does not shy away from honestly confronting the heartbreaking aspects of life with a child who has a terminal disease, including many levels of loss. *Kirkus Reviews*

A moving account of a remarkable young man and his supportive family battling Duchenne muscular dystrophy. Kirkus Reviews

This is such a personal and important project. I can't imagine how challenging it must have been to write about Riley's journey and the reality of living with Duchenne. *Richard Faleti*

Congratulations on the release of your latest book! Your innovative approach and compelling storytelling are sure to resonate with readers and make a significant impact in the literary world. *Agbaje Morenikeji*

Congratulations!! Love it. The story is very compelling. *Hilda Irons*

It's amazing that you're sharing Riley's journey with the world, shedding light on Duchenne Muscular Dystrophy. ... Thank you for bringing attention to such an important topic. *Eduards Vars*

January 2024
Dianne's Consultant Services
Anaheim, CA

ISBN: 979-8-9896649-1-7 Paperback
ISBN: 979-8-9905196-6-4 eBook

Table of Contents

Foreword

By Greg Stuart

When my sister Nina, my youngest sibling who is 8 years younger than myself, first informed me that she was writing a book about her son Riley, I felt it would be a literary success. Now, having just finished reading the book, my initial predictions have been confirmed and exceeded. *The Life of Riley* is a compelling narrative about Riley Herrera's battle against *Duchenne muscular dystrophy (DMD)* and his relationships with his family members. The single most important relationship is with his mother, who is also his number one caregiver. The importance of a bond between a mother and child can never be overstated, but when the child is rendered disabled because of a life-threatening disease, this bond greatly intensifies and becomes difficult to put into its proper context. Mere words fail on most occasions to do it justice. Yet, the author's attempt throughout this book to accurately convey to the reader a real sense of the emotions felt between the two isn't just admirable but is highly successful.

My life experiences have given me the ability to provide a unique and qualified perspective on Riley's life. I'm Nina's (Riley's mother) oldest brother, Greg, who, like Riley, is afflicted with a neuromuscular disorder. I have been confined to a wheelchair for 45 years and require assistance from others to perform the simplest of daily tasks. I have often opined that people should never take the ability to tie their shoes for granted. Riley commented that when you're being dressed by somebody else, the goal is never to look like a committee has put you together. Riley never failed to appreciate that his mom and dad did the best they could under the most difficult of circumstances.

My sister makes it abundantly clear that our family became stronger because of the hardships we encountered, but in the end, we truly found grace because we participated in Riley's life.

Dianne DeMille, Ph.D. and Nina Stuart Herrera

Introduction

The book is titled *The Life of Riley: Living with Duchenne Muscular Dystrophy* because it encapsulates the extraordinary life of someone who has faced immense challenges at a young age. Riley never gave up or lost hope that we would find a way to keep him going. It has been 31 years in the making because it took this long for Riley to allow us to write it.

This story is not just about Riley's journey; it encompasses our journey as a family and how we grew alongside him, learning to understand his disease. I am Nina Stuart Herrera, Riley's mother, and I am joined by Dianne DeMille, who helped pen this book through a mother's eyes.

Two of my brothers were diagnosed with *Spinal muscular atrophy (SMA)* at a young age and are still thriving. Greg is 62, and Dave is 59 years old. My son, Riley, turned 31 on April 11, 2023, battling *Duchenne muscular dystrophy (DMD)*. It is nothing short of a miracle. Their strength, courage, and unwavering determination to live life to the fullest under any circumstances have made it all possible.

What makes this story truly unique is that it involves two debilitating diseases affecting two generations of the same family, both with a prognosis of premature death. Doctors told us that the chances of having two types of *muscular dystrophy* in one family are "one in a million."

This story is also about unconditional love. It is about having faith in human beings' ability to overcome insurmountable odds. My parents' unconditional love for all of us drove them to go the extra mile, especially during an era when the resources we have today were not available.

Our daughter, Alexis, whom we affectionately call Lexi, plays a significant role in our lives and is integral to Riley's story. She is now 30 years old and received a degree in nursing from *Grand Canyon University*.

Riley wants to be known simply as Riley, not as the boy with a heart transplant or the man with *DMD*. I want to emphasize that he is an extraordinary human being who desires nothing more than to live an ordinary life. Who would have thought that Riley could survive a heart transplant? He doesn't consider himself a hero but seeks to inspire other boys diagnosed with *DMD* to live long and fulfilling lives. It has been 17 years since Riley's transplant, and he is now ready for us to share his story. Enough time has passed, and most of the emotional and medical scars have healed. We have reached a point where we can reflect on the past while keeping a keen eye on the future. He deserves immense credit for wanting to share his story with the world.

DMD is like a ticking time bomb, leaving families uncertain about their child's future. However, we hope for a day when the word "incurable" is replaced with "curable." *The Life of Riley* tells the story of a child who defied all odds. After all these years, our lives are still filled with hope and vitality. We have never given up on Riley, and he has never given up on himself. Through this book, we aim to help others learn from our mistakes and triumphs.

Riley's journey would have been impossible without the extraordinary individuals who supported him. We have conducted interviews with my brothers Greg and Dave, and Pat Furlong, Founding President and CEO of *Parent Project Muscular Dystrophy (PPMD),* the largest nonprofit organization in the United States dedicated to improving the treatment, quality of life, and long-term care for all affected by *DMD.* Insights from Dr. Linda Cripe, a distinguished professor of pediatrics and pediatric cardiologist, along with many others, have profoundly influenced Riley's life.

It is my goal to do this book justice. It holds deep personal significance for me as I strive to convey Riley's extraordinary saga to the reader.

Acknowledgments

Shout out to Oprah Winfrey! This book would never have been written without her, and she doesn't even know it! You see, Dianne DeMille, the co-author of this book, had previously co-written another book called *Path of the Devil*. Dianne had sent Oprah an autographed copy of that book, but unfortunately, it was returned and ended up in Amazon's used bookstore. It was purely serendipitous that my husband, Ron, happened to purchase that same autographed copy through the used bookstore. When he opened the book, he discovered that Dianne had written a personal message to Oprah. The inscription read, "To Oprah, One of my favorite people!" -- Dr. Dianne DeMille.

After Ron discovered this, he reached out to Dianne to return the book to her. Their conversation led to our connection, and the rest is history. Fate brought Dianne and me together, and by the grace of God, she decided to embark on this journey with me.

I want to express my heartfelt gratitude to Oprah for unknowingly playing a crucial role in bringing us together. Thank you for being the go-between you never knew you were.

Chapter 1: Becoming Riley's Parents

Nina: Growing up in Butte, Montana

This chapter is dedicated to my parents, who I consider to be the most heroic people I have ever met. I don't think I would be living my life the way I do today without growing up and having the experience of being the little sister and my parent's youngest child. We interviewed Greg and Dave about their diagnosis and growing up with Spinal muscular atrophy (*SMA*). Mom and Dad are both deceased as we write this story.

Born 1969 – Living a Normal Life

I was born in 1969 in Butte, Montana, the youngest of five children. My childhood prepared me for the journey of raising my own children, Riley and Alexis (Lexi). *SMA*, a form of *muscular dystrophy*, has stricken two of my brothers. It is a genetic disease that impacts the central nervous system and all the muscles in the body. As a result, both of my brothers experienced a decline in strength and are now confined to wheelchairs. They are currently 58 and 61 years old. Living with this disease in my family helped prepare me to care for Riley and become who I am today.

Back: Nina, Chris, Maria
Front: Dave, Greg

I always remember having a happy and normal childhood. My mother, Mary, had five children within nine years. Maria was the oldest, and I was the youngest, with my three brothers, Greg, Dave, and Chris, between us. The nine-year age gap between Maria and me created a unique family dynamic, with my sister often taking care of me when I was young. I remember Mom telling me that Maria was thrilled to have another girl in the family and treated me like her own.

1

My parents dedicated a great deal of time trying to understand and diagnose Greg and Dave's condition. While they took my brothers on trips for medical evaluations and treatments, my sister stayed behind and played a critical role in my upbringing before moving out of the house at the age of 19. During these experiences, I learned valuable life lessons and developed the resilience needed to navigate life's challenges.

Looking back, I can say that I had a somewhat idyllic upbringing. Despite the presence of *SMA* in our family, we were raised with a profound respect for life and an understanding that we should make the most of it. This mindset is what makes our story unique.

My mother, Mary, and father, Howard Stuart, were highly educated. My mom earned her bachelor's degrees in history and political science, followed by a master's degree in Spanish from the University of Montana. Dad majored in English and Latin at the University of Montana and later obtained a master's degree in special education from San Francisco State University. Their educational backgrounds proved invaluable when making difficult decisions regarding my brothers' health.

I learned a lot from my parents about how to raise a child with a debilitating disease. It was not about keeping up with societal expectations but rather about staying true to oneself and creating a safe, happy, nurtured, and respected environment for our family.

We were raised in a faithful Catholic household, attending church every Sunday and participating in sacraments such as baptism, First Communion, and Confirmation. My mother even taught the catechism class we attended. Faith played a significant role in helping us navigate the challenges of our family tragedy, instilling in us the belief in a higher power and the hope it brings.

I quickly learned the importance of facing adversity head-on and finding strength even in the toughest times. When Greg and Dave were going through their diagnosis with my parents, I was much younger and somewhat shielded from the full impact. As a family, we strived for normalcy and believed life would go as usual. My mom was a superwoman, and my dad worked as a school principal. Both had a deep compassion for helping others. If anyone could handle the challenges we faced, it was them. We learned that having a disability should not hinder one's happiness or the pursuit of goals. Little did I know that these experiences were preparing me for the journey of caring for Riley.

Despite the hardships we faced, I always felt loved and cared for. *SMA* did not define us as a family; instead, we carried on with our lives and refused to let it hold us back. We possessed the strength and knowledge to overcome any obstacles that came our way. My parents were firm yet supportive, always believing that we could handle whatever life threw at us. In times of difficulty, we understood the importance of lifting ourselves up and seeking a helping hand rather than handouts. These values and lessons would ultimately make a tremendous difference in my life as I embarked on the challenge of caring for Riley.

Brothers diagnosed with Spinal Muscular Atrophy (SMA)

My older brother, Greg, began experiencing difficulty walking upstairs when he was five years old. Concerned, my mom took him to a doctor in Butte, Montana. Unfortunately, they dismissed his symptoms as a ploy for attention. As my younger brother Chris grew older, my parents noticed that he, too, had trouble walking and was bow-legged. He was fitted with braces to correct his leg alignment, but *SMA* did not affect him.

Dave, my middle brother, was a different story altogether. Dave grew up being a rough-and-tumble-star athlete who wouldn't let anything get in his way. He was a resilient and determined individual, excelling in sports and overcoming any obstacles in his path. Our parents instilled this resilience in us, raised us to be independent thinkers, and encouraged us to overcome challenges. They raised us to find ways to cope and be productive human beings. We were taught not to let anything stand in the way of achieving our goals. However, as Dave hit puberty, he began encountering issues related to *SMA*.

I distinctly remember observing how my brothers supported each other during this challenging period. Due to the age difference and gender dynamics, I wasn't actively involved, but I witnessed the bond between them.

3

Finally, Greg received an accurate diagnosis when he was ten years old. He underwent testing at the *Mayo Clinic* in Rochester, Minnesota, where he was correctly diagnosed with *Spinal muscular atrophy Type 3*, also known as *Kugelberg-Welander Disease*. In contrast, Dave's symptoms did not surface until later in his adolescence, and he was diagnosed with late-onset *SMA*. The progression of *SMA* has been different for each of my brothers.

When I interviewed Greg about how our mother realized something was wrong with him, he recounted, "I think she became aware of it through our neighbors, who noticed that I walked in an unusual or funny manner. They described my gait as bear-like. After hearing their observations, my mom began paying closer attention to my walking. She always had a keen eye and intuitive sense about her children and could detect when something was off."

So, thus began the journey of her taking Greg to see multiple doctors to find out what was going on. Greg recalls, "One doctor told her I was lazy, and the other said I just wanted attention."

It's important to note that these events took place in the 1960s and 1970s when medical knowledge and resources concerning muscular disorders were not as advanced as they are today.

Greg continued, "At that time, my parents were in the dark and quite unaware of *SMA*, and the available resources in Montana were limited. There was insufficient research on the disease and its treatments. Consequently, my parents had to travel out of state to Seattle and Salt Lake City for my testing. We were all very young, and my memories of those times are hazy. I can only imagine the challenges my parents faced due to the lack of support and resources. Nevertheless, they did everything they could for me under those difficult circumstances."

My parents took Greg to the University of Utah, where he underwent a biopsy. The biopsy results were inconclusive, providing no definitive answer about Greg's condition. Some speculated that he might have *Duchenne muscular dystrophy* (*DMD*), but the university medical professionals acknowledged the presence of a muscular disorder without being able to identify it conclusively. They told my parents, "We know you have a muscular disorder, but we're not sure what it is because the biopsy was inconclusive," and so he was sent home.

Greg continues, "Finally, when I turned ten, my mom took me to our local pediatrician, Dr. Gillespie. His son, who was also a doctor, had connections at the *Mayo Clinic*. Dr. Gillespie facilitated an appointment for me, emphasizing the need to identify and obtain confirmation of my condition. I met with a renowned neurologist named Dr. Mellinger at the *Mayo Clinic*. Within two days of testing, he identified that I had *Spinal muscular atrophy* Type 3, specifically *Kugelberg-Welander Disease* (juvenile *SMA*). He explained that it was caused by both parents carrying an autosomal recessive gene. In this case, my father had the autosomal recessive gene, and my mother carried the same gene. Out of our five siblings, Dave and I inherited the disease, whilst Maria, Chris, and Nina were spared."

Greg reflected, "Throughout this entire process, my parents did not suspect anything was wrong with Dave since he was a talented athlete and showed no signs of *SMA*. Instead, when they visited multiple doctors including an orthopedist, they brought Chris, who was experiencing difficulties with walking. As it turned out, Chris was bow-legged and pigeon-toed, requiring orthopedic shoes and a brace at night to correct his foot alignment. Little did they know that Dave, silently affected by *SMA*, was lurking in the shadows."

Growing up, Greg and Dave shared a deep bond. Dave recognized the challenges Greg faced and understood that he, too, had *SMA*. Dave said, "I looked up to my brother and thought he has it much worse than me since it began at such an early age for him, while mine surfaced later. If he can endure it, so can I. That's how I approached it."

Muscle weakness progresses differently in individuals with *SMA* type 3. Some may lose the ability to walk during adolescence, while others can continue walking well into adulthood. Various factors, such as growth spurts during the teenage years or a late-onset *SMA* diagnosis, like in Dave's case, can affect the progression of the disease.

Dave recounts, "I started noticing something was wrong when I was around 11 years old. I was showing signs of the disease. Despite being a big kid and developing early, I could still keep up with other kids in the neighborhood and at school. I didn't think much of it, and nobody in my family mentioned anything to me. Towards the end of fifth grade, I started realizing that I wasn't as fast or as good as I used to be."

His older brother Greg remembers, "I knew something was wrong even before our parents because I could see it when Dave ran, although he was still faster than most kids. I noticed a slight glitch or stiffness in his leg."

Dave continues, "I was still hanging in there in sixth grade. I was the quarterback of the football team and played basketball. But I could feel something happening to my body. I didn't mention it to our parents because I didn't think they could handle having two boys with the same disease. By seventh grade, when I started playing football, there were only two people slower than me, and they were much heavier. It was a tough transition during my formative years. It felt like I was going from hero to zero, just like that."

Dave recalls an incident when he watched Greg try to play basketball in seventh grade. Greg was dragging himself up and down the court. A teacher who was watching the game approached my mom and said, "He drags himself up and down the court. He is the most courageous person I have ever met."

My family grew up in the small mining town of Butte, Montana, so we learned to be tough and resilient. That's just how we were raised, and we tried to live life as normally as possible. Dave looked up to Greg, who faced the disease with such grace and dignity despite having so much trouble. Dave thought, "Wow! Greg has something special, and if he can do it, I can do it, too."

Dave watched Greg navigate through the disease and thought, "I'm starting to feel it, too. Growing up in Butte, you were expected to be tough. You just dealt with it, sucked it up, and moved forward. That's exactly what I did, without compromise. No quarter taken, none given."

When Dave was 12 years old, my parents decided to take him to a *Muscular Dystrophy Association* (*MDA*) clinic in Billings, Montana, for testing. By then, Dave believed his parents already had an idea of what was going on since they would conduct some tests on him. They had all the paperwork from the *Mayo Clinic*, so they must have known. The doctor confirmed, "Oh yeah, Dave definitely has the same thing."

Dave remembers Mom saying, "The day they found out, Dad went outside and threw up. This was his second son."

Reflecting on his father's reaction, Dave says, "My old man was not an emotional person. He grew up in Butte, Montana, and went through World War II. On the other hand, Mom grew up tough as nails on a ranch in Little Basin, on the outskirts of Butte. But that day, my dad showed his emotions. My mom told me she had never seen him act like that before, and he had let it all out."

Greg chimes in, "My father, a realist, sometimes bordered on fatalism. He believed that when things happen, you have to accept them. That's life! He kept his emotions hidden. There were things about his military service that we never knew. He would just let out a little bit at a time. For instance, one of his buddies came through town years later and stayed with Mom and Dad when we were children. This buddy told Mom about the Bronze Star and other medals my dad had received. She said, 'Dad never even asked for it.' It wasn't until he was in his early 80s that my brothers and I talked to him about the Bronze Star, which he had never claimed. Mom said, 'You better claim it because your sons might like it. Or you might want to pass it down.'"

"On the other hand, my mother was more expressive and outgoing. She was relentless in advocating for my brothers. If she wasn't satisfied with an answer, she would persist until she found a better one. Many doctors labeled her as 'abrasive' or 'difficult,' but she would respond, 'Yes, I am. I'm determined to find the right answer.' During that time, limited information was available about *SMA* (*Spinal muscular atrophy*). So, when they discovered that Dave also had the condition, my father's emotional side emerged. That was the end of it for him. He let it all out and said, 'We have another son like this. We need to get on with life.'"

Parents — Coping

Our parents had a strong Catholic faith, which played a significant role in our upbringing and helped us move forward as a family.

Greg stated, "The people in Butte had grit and spirit. Everyone stuck together. Our grandfather, David Andrew Stuart, who was our dad's father, worked as a copper miner thousands of feet underground. It was a dangerous job, and there were incidents where hundreds of people lost their lives. Mom had a tough life, and it was even tougher for her mother, Birdie Gennara."

Greg continues, "Birdie, our grandma, was French Canadian and lived in a French-Canadian community outside Butte. Her father ran a sawmill there. Her grandfather immigrated from Maza di Vigo, Tyrol, Italy, when he was 16 years old. He passed Ellis Island with $16 hidden in his underwear. He couldn't speak the language and ended up in Michigan because his brother lived there and worked in the mines. Then, he decided to move to Butte because there was more money working in the copper mines. He homesteaded a place in little Basin Creek, six to seven miles outside the city. It was a small ranch, but he and my grandmother cleared all the rocks out of there and made it livable, where they could grow some hay. Mom told us about not having indoor plumbing until she turned 13."

Dave went on, "On my father's side, it was all about mining. Both parents wanted a better life for their children than they had experienced. It's natural for parents to desire the best for their children, and even at that time, my parents had the opportunity to choose education."

"Through it all, there was always their faith. Mom grew up with a strong Catholic faith, and when she was young, Grandpa built their new house with a little chapel, including pews and a stained-glass window, so they could pray and say the Rosary. Dad grew up in a very strong Baptist family. Religion became the main focal point for our upbringing."

Greg continues, "Before meeting my mom, my dad converted from being a Baptist to Catholicism. He had a thirst for knowledge and studied various religions. Eventually, he decided to convert to Catholicism. While growing up, my dad didn't impose religion on us, but he would take communion every day. However, my mom played a more active role. Both had a strong Catholic faith, and my mom taught us CCD. We were all baptized, received our First Holy Communion, and went through confirmation. All of us, except my oldest sister Maria, graduated from Butte Central Catholic High School."

"When they married, my mom focused on caring for the children and staying at home. We were one of the few Catholic families in the neighborhood. During that time, it was common for women to stay at home while the men went out to work, even if it meant working multiple jobs."

Greg recalled a story from when he was around six years old. He said, "At that time, my dad was teaching at Harrison School, instructing fifth and sixth graders. After a full day of teaching, he would come home at 4:00 PM, quickly grab his dinner packed in a lunch pail, and head off to work at the railroad as a clerk. This routine continued for quite some time. He even worked at the railroad during many Christmases. After a few years, he stopped working there and focused solely on education, becoming a principal, which meant he didn't have to work at the railroad anymore. Even though my mom obtained her master's degree in Spanish, and they were both well-educated for that time, they divided their duties. Mom stayed at home and made sure everyone's needs were met."

My parents had a deep love for children, and their strong faith prepared them for the challenges that came with having children, especially two with *SMA*. My mom fought to keep my brothers in regular classrooms for school. Greg had difficulty walking due to his *SMA*, so whenever he faced any problems at school, my parents were there to support him. If he fell, the school would call home, and one of my parents would rush to be there for him.

They were determined to make things work, regardless of the sacrifices they had to make, because they understood the importance of education for Greg and Dave's future. My mom did everything in her power to ensure we had the same opportunities and advantages as anyone else.

9

Their faith and hope gave them the strength to overcome obstacles, but it wasn't without struggle and constant vigilance.

Greg shared a significant moment in his life when a tough decision had to be made. He remembered being 13 years old and experiencing difficulty walking. Both he and Mom noticed that his feet would turn out while walking. Greg initially thought it was absurd, thinking, "I'm too young for this."

Mom shared the same concern and took him to consult with doctors in Billings, Montana. The doctors weren't sure what to do until they came across an orthopedist who suggested using plastic braces instead of metal ones, as the latter would be too heavy for Greg to walk with. He wore plastic braces that extended below the knee, which helped him maintain his ability to walk. His goal was to keep walking until he graduated from high school.

Greg was a straight-A–student who excelled academically. When it was time for him to start high school, the school wanted to place him in the Special Education or Resource program on the first floor. My parents firmly believed that Greg didn't belong in those programs and deserved the education he was capable of.

The public high school informed my parents that they couldn't accommodate Greg because they didn't have an elevator and wouldn't rearrange his classes to meet his needs.

Mom responded, "Well, that won't work. He's a bright kid, and if you won't do this for him, I will find another way to ensure he receives what he needs."

She turned to the Catholic school, named Butte Central High School, where they assured her that Greg would have access to the elevator and that they would accommodate him in any way possible. My mom made it happen because she was a determined go-getter who never took no for an answer.

Mom and Dad believed in the public education system because they were both educators, so we began going to public school. When Greg's situation arose, Mom said the high school had no elevator and couldn't accommodate physically disabled people. So, Greg went to Butte Central

Catholic High School as a freshman. He was just physically disabled, not mentally disabled, and could learn just as well as other students.

Greg remained at Butte Central High School because they had the necessary accessibility features, and the staff went out of their way to accommodate him. This willingness to help may have been influenced by the religious training they received, particularly from Brother McCormick, a Christian Brothers of Ireland member, who always looked out for Greg and ensured his needs were being met.

Today, there would be a lawsuit. Everything is accessible now that the American Disabilities Act exists. Back then, in 1976, they didn't have that and didn't push for it.

Greg recalls, "After a while, our mother saw that it was the religious belief and principles she wanted us to have. The Catholic School would accommodate anybody, come hell or high water. Public schools weren't forced by law to do anything at the time. The Catholic school just took it upon themselves. It was an elevator that only the nuns could use, and they allowed me to use it. They would move classes around to accommodate me. They helped people, and that's what the Catholic Church did. Many people working in Catholic charities and in Catholic education do a lot of good around the world. For all the bad news you hear about it, many good people don't get the publicity and are overshadowed by the sensational headlines of a few bad apples who do unspeakable things. Maybe sometimes we need to focus on that part that has a valuable purpose and meaning in our society. I will always be eternally grateful to them."

Dave also recalls his positive experience at Butte Central. "Everything was going well with Greg, so they decided to send me to Butte Central. I had trouble at times, but I didn't require an elevator, and I could easily attend all my classes and navigate the stairs. The accommodations, including the elevator, were in place just in case. Butte Central had shown dedication for their students, regardless of their disability."

Mom and Dad decided to send Chris and me to the same private Catholic school despite the financial strain the tuition imposed on them. They believed in the importance of education and actively engaged with the school to make it possible for each of their children to receive a quality education. My oldest sister, Maria, stayed in the public high school, Butte High, because she was already established and had her friends there. My parents didn't want to make it harder on her than necessary.

Greg achieved the goal he had set for himself. He walked at graduation and accepted his diploma from Butte Central in 1979. Dave followed in his footsteps and graduated in 1983 while still walking!!! Chris and I soon followed, with him graduating in 1985 and me in 1987. My oldest sister, Maria, graduated from Butte High in 1978.

Mother involved with MDA Telethons

My mother had a deep interest in understanding the condition affecting her sons and sought the best strategies and the latest information available. The *Muscular Dystrophy Association* (*MDA*) was the primary source of information on the disease. In her quest for knowledge and to support Greg, who was diagnosed with *Spinal muscular atrophy* (*SMA*), she began working with *MDA* during their annual *Labor Day Telethon*. This involvement started before they discovered that Dave also had *SMA*. She had an insatiable appetite for learning and would relentlessly pursue answers, refusing to accept "No" as an answer. Her determination stemmed from a desire to find a cure.

Working with *MDA* was particularly beneficial for my mom because they played a vital role when Greg and Dave transitioned to using wheelchairs. *MDA* provided assistance with various equipment needs, including covering the cost of wheelchairs and adaptive devices. Eventually, other organizations and government programs began to assume these financial responsibilities, such as insurance coverage or Medicare. However, parents and *MDA* supporters continued to advocate for more research and tangible results, as they were dedicated to finding a cure and were unsatisfied with the progress.

There have been real breakthroughs with *Spinal muscular atrophy* (*SMA*) in recent years. Greg and Dave, however, are over a generation too late. For children today, the outlook is much brighter due to increased funding and research conducted by various organizations, including *MDA*.

These advancements generate excitement as they offer potential cures or treatments to manage the condition. Although some research efforts have encountered setbacks, there have been notable breakthroughs, and organizations like the *MDA* have emphasized the need for visible results and treatments that can slow down disease progression.

I remember Mom being the constant presence whenever something related to *SMA* occurred. She tirelessly pursued any available research and even reached out to Senators and members of Congress to advocate for wheelchair accessibility and other necessary equipment, not only for her sons but for anyone who needed them. Her involvement in the *MDA* telethons was driven by a belief in the importance of providing support to individuals with disabilities. She felt that it was important for everyone to have a chance at a normal life, even with a terminal disease.

I can relate to her experiences based on my own personal insight. People often look at Riley and assume he is fine, but they don't truly understand or experience what it's like to live with him daily. They don't know what challenges we face or what doctors have told us.

As Dave and Greg grew older, Mom made the decision to stop working the annual *Labor Day MDA Telethons*. However, that didn't mean she stopped fighting for her boys. She always figured out a way to make anything happen if they ever needed anything.

When we discovered Riley's specific disease, Ron and I turned to the *Parent Project Muscular Dystrophy* (*PPMD*) because they had started their own grassroots organization focused on conducting research for *Duchenne* and *Becker muscular dystrophy*. We needed more detailed information about Duchenne's with over 40 conditions under the MDA umbrella.

It takes a lot of strength and courage to fight for your child and be such a strong advocate. My mom and dad were truly superhuman in their quest to learn everything they could to help my brothers and find the best available support and equipment for them to lead productive lives. Greg used leg braces for several years before eventually transitioning to a wheelchair, just like Dave. Our parents worked tirelessly around the clock.

Whenever they needed assistance, they made sure we were involved, and we did our best to help. These experiences prepared me for what I needed to do for Riley. I can only imagine how difficult it must have been for them to raise five children, let alone two boys with *SMA*. They had to navigate the challenges of finding out what they had, getting a proper diagnosis, and traveling out of state for medical appointments.

Montana was an underserved state and still is today. The state didn't have the resources to provide proper care or diagnosis to meet my brother's needs. They were misdiagnosed several times, and it was only when my parents sought answers out of state that they received a correct diagnosis at the *Mayo Clinic*. I remember everything Mom and Dad did for them. Mom was constantly researching, making phone calls, and arranging for tests to be done. Sometimes, our parents had to take turns taking Greg to different hospitals and appointments. And when they both had to go, they had to find someone to care for the rest of us at home. They relied on the support of family and friends to bridge the gap. We faced similar challenges with Riley and Lexi when they were young. I know Mom had support, but it was still difficult with school and other activities.

My parents weren't afraid to take risks when it came to helping Greg. They were willing to try anything new and listen to any advice that was given to them. Like my parents, Greg was determined to have a normal life and learn how to live with his disease. Greg was fully on board, and Riley reminds me a lot of him.

I have vivid memories of Greg in high school. He desperately wanted to get his driver's license, and since he was still able to walk at that time, he could qualify. The only problem was that Greg couldn't lift his leg to go from the gas pedal to the brake. Mom researched, bought him hand controls, and had them installed in the car. Mom and Dad were overjoyed that Greg had found a sense of independence.

Life was far from easy, but my parents did their best and stayed committed to each other. With this disease, many couples end up getting divorced. Usually, one partner can't handle the stress, while the other doesn't want to put in the effort. I suppose that's where I get my determination.

I also remember when Dad was working as a principal, and as Greg got older, it became increasingly challenging for him to get out of bed. Dad would come home during his lunch break to get my brother out of bed and dressed for the day. They deserve as much praise as anyone for their unwavering strength and perseverance. Many people simply give up.

Another memory that sticks out in my mind is when I went down to the basement as an adult long after I had moved out of the house. We rarely had a reason to go down there because Greg and Dave could no longer use it, so it was essentially abandoned. I peeked into one of the empty rooms and saw plastic braces, walkers, wheelchairs, old commodes, and so on. It was a stark reminder of just how much Mom and Dad did to make life easier for my brothers. This was just one example of the time and effort they put in to keep them going.

In retrospect, I know my parents were under a tremendous amount of stress, but they tried not to let it show. They instilled in my brothers and me the belief that we shouldn't feel sorry for ourselves. They taught us that feeling sorry for oneself consumes valuable time and energy and ultimately serves no purpose. My brothers would often tell Riley, "You are who you are, and don't blame anyone for your problems. It is what it is, and you always need to keep moving forward."

Riley has been living with this terminal disease for many years, yet he is still moving forward at the age of 31.

Brothers Began Using Wheelchairs and Learning to Cope

At the age of 17, Greg became confined to a wheelchair. Determined to pursue higher education, he expressed his desire to attend college at 18. Recognizing the importance of education in his life, our parents wholeheartedly supported him, saying, "We must make this a reality for him. He deserves an education."

Greg set his sights on Montana State University in Bozeman despite having a local college option in Butte. He yearned for independence and the opportunity to meet new people. Mom and Dad always encouraged us not to be afraid to take chances. Encouraging his independence, Mom and Dad accompanied Greg on a college tour in Bozeman. Greg aspired to live in the dorms and engage in social activities. Everything seemed in place, except for the fact that he required assistance due to his being in a wheelchair. My mom diligently reached out to various agencies and successfully found a suitable caregiver for Greg.

Mom told me how she and Dad dropped Greg off at the university. They were both full of pride, yet scared to death, thinking about how he would survive. They all took a huge leap of faith that day, which paid off. Greg graduated from Montana State University in Bozeman with a bachelor's degree in psychology.

During Greg's time at MSU, our parents' faith faced another test. Our eldest sister, Maria, got married at 19 and had a child the following year. It was an exciting yet anxiety-inducing period for my parents. Since Maria hadn't undergone genetic testing yet, nobody knew if she carried the gene for SMA. This uncharted territory brought forth mixed emotions for our parents throughout her pregnancy.

It was an exciting and terrifying time in their lives. The prospect of my parents being grandparents should be a wondrous and happy time. For my mom and dad, this was also a time of extreme anxiety and concern for their unborn grandchild.

Nevertheless, their unwavering, steadfast faith held our family together. They possessed enough hope and belief for all of us, regardless of the circumstances. As a family, we were confident that we could overcome any challenges that lay ahead. We could get through this and survive! My sister knew she could rely on our parents for ongoing support. At 20 years old, Maria gave birth to our parents' first grandchild, a grandson named Robert Howard Tromly, whose middle name was after my father.

While filled with excitement at the arrival of this new bundle of joy, my parents were petrified because he was a boy. Given our family's history, there were concerns. Throughout his formative years, Mom and Dad kept a watchful eye on Robert's development and were relieved to see no signs of SMA. No matter how many times our family's faith was tested, our belief in God always carried us through. My sister hit the jackpot because Robert turned out perfectly fine!!!

Creating His Own Path

Upon graduating from MSU, Greg returned home to live with us once again. Restless and eager to leave the parental nest once again, he found an ally in Chris, who was graduating from high school at the time. Chris, the youngest boy in our family, always looked up to his older brothers. They shared a strong brotherly bond, and Chris wanted to attend the University of Montana after high school in 1985. Chris played an integral part in the next chapter of Greg's life, allowing him to complete his second degree.

Greg, desiring a career change, decided to pursue a degree in accounting. Chris agreed to care for Greg while they both attended the University of Montana together.

I hold immense respect and pride for Chris, who enabled his older brother to pursue his passion. Balancing both responsibilities requires significant time and energy, yet Chris embraced it effortlessly. It exemplifies the unique bond within our family, always there for each other through thick and thin. Chris pursued a degree in business finance, while Greg obtained his bachelor's in accounting.

Making New Memories

At the age of 26, my brother Dave defied the limitations of SMA. He still walked without devices or braces He wasn't going to allow anyone or any disease bring him down. Despite the disease, he remained an adventurous spirit. Dave attended community college for a while and later moved to Salt Lake City with a friend to seek employment. During those years of studying and working, he never asked our parents for assistance. He still had mobility, could drive without medical equipment, and held a full-time job. However, when he decided to move back to Butte for short stint because he was between jobs; this decision would change his life forever.

One day, while driving with our cousin, they were struck head-on by a drunk driver who had passed out with her foot on the gas pedal. Fortunately, a passerby rescued Dave and our cousin just before their car burst into flames.

Their lives were saved, but Dave suffered a broken femur and collapsed lungs. Our cousin also broke his femur. Mom was beside herself with worry. The doctor performed surgery on Dave's broken femur, making an incision along the entire length and inserting a rod. The procedure required cutting into the muscle, leaving Mom horrified and wondering about his future mobility.

Despite walking with crutches for another six years, Dave never gave up. He refused to succumb to a wheelchair until he turned 32. We later discovered that if he had undergone surgery using new techniques available at a different hospital, he might have enjoyed three to four more years of walking.

After the accident, all three brothers returned home to live under one roof with our parents. Greg and Chris had just graduated from the University of Montana and Dave was up for a new adventure. They hatched a plan and decided to all move to Las Vegas. I could tell my parents were nervous, but Greg and Dave were determined. With Chris caring for Greg and assisting Dave when needed, they again had faith and hoped things would work out. They bought a red Nissan truck. The day they left, Chris transferred Greg into the truck, followed by Dave, who tossed the wheelchair in the back. They left and never looked back.

I look back on this memory with awe. We had a family dynamic like no other. It takes a lot of sacrifice to do what Chris did. It also takes hope and faith to believe things will work out. Chris helped Greg and Dave as much as they helped him. Love is powerful and makes you do things so others can live.

Dave recalls, "Greg tried to live as normal a life as possible. [turning to Greg] You went out and did it. That was you [talking to Greg], and everybody knew it, no matter how many struggles there were. My condition went differently. We had the same thing, but we reacted differently. I honestly believe it took more years to beat me down. Don't you, Greg?"

"I agree. I think it's obvious. It's just a matter of time before it does take you down."

Having *SMA*, they both succumbed to the wheelchair, but that doesn't mean the fight isn't over. *SMA* may have won the battle, but my brothers are still fighting the war!

Genetic Testing for Nina

When I was 10 years old, my older sister Maria got married. She had not been tested for the SMA gene before giving birth, which would have been a tough lesson for my mom and dad to learn.

When I turned 18, Mom and Dad decided it was vital for me to know if I carried the autosomal recessive gene that causes *SMA*. It wasn't about the disability but about being prepared for what might be necessary. My parents were going to make sure I was equipped with all the proper tools available for me to make informed decisions about my body. The only hospital in the area that could do the testing was Shodair Children's Hospital in Helena, Montana.

In 1987, I went for genetic testing and counseling. I wanted to understand the possibilities should I decide to have children. The tests came back that I carried the gene for *SMA*. I was then informed that to have a child with *SMA*, I would have to get pregnant by someone who also carried the autosomal recessive gene.

There was still a lot of uncertainty, and I received counseling that the chances of having a child with *SMA* were not significant enough to worry about having or not having children. They still didn't know much about what my brothers had, except that they would not have longevity. We were crashing through barriers at every turn.

Ron: Growing up in East Helena, Montana

My husband, Ron, grew up in a family similar to mine. We were both the youngest of five children and grew up in a blue-collar town. Ron's hometown was East Helena, Montana, where he was raised by his parents, Gustavo and Inge Herrera.

Ron's dad, Gustavo Herrera, was born in Lima, Peru. He immigrated to the United States in his 20s, became a US citizen, and served in the Korean War. He pursued a degree in chemical engineering at Louisiana State University. One of his first jobs was for Asarco in East Helena, Montana. Ron's mother, Ingeborg Ahlers, was born in Kempten, Germany, and immigrated to the United States in her 20s and became a US citizen. She dedicated her time to taking care of the children.

Ron's parents met at a social gathering and got married in East Helena, Montana. He grew up as part of a first-generation American family alongside his four siblings: Lisa, Dan, Rick, and Steve.

Ron had a happy and typical upbringing, instilled with strong family values. The family was raised Catholic, and Ron has carried this belief throughout his life. His strong faith has carried us through some of the most difficult time in our lives.

Ron was surrounded by his four siblings and enjoyed all of Montana's outdoor activities. When he was young, his family purchased a cabin in Canyon Ferry, just outside Helena, Montana. His mom would tell him the mountains reminded her of the Alps, where she grew up in Germany. They spent a lot of time boating and swimming as a family at the lake. They also skied in the wintertime. His Dad's great love of the outdoors brought him to teach Ron and his 3 brothers how to hunt. Ron has passed his love of hunting on to Riley and his passion for skiing to Lexi.

Ron's love for his parents has never faded, and he continues to tell Riley and Lexi new things about them every chance he has. His father, Gustavo, died when Ron was just 19 years old, at 56. Riley, Lexi and I never got to meet him but feel like we know him through Ron's stories.

Ron's mother, Inge, passed away at age 67. Riley was seven, and Lexi was five. They have fond memories of when she babysat for them. They called her Omi, German for grandmother.

Nina and Ron, The Early Years

I met Ron in June 1991 at a bar/restaurant called Riley's, located at Canyon Ferry Lake in Helena, Montana. Ron was 25 years old at the time, and I was 22. I was staying at my older sister Maria's cabin, which she owned with her husband Bill, while Ron was staying at his family's cabin. He was shy, and being my outgoing self, I immediately introduced myself to him. I thought he was cute, and I was drawn to his personality.

How Ron and I met is an integral part of our story because it exemplifies the strength and character we both possessed when it came to raising Riley and determining the best course of action. We were young and faced challenging circumstances.

Ron had recently graduated from Montana State University with a finance degree in 1990. He had just started working for the federal government. He was about to undergo training to become a special agent for the Criminal Investigation Division (CID) of the Treasury Department.

In 1991, I graduated from Western Montana University with a bachelor's degree in elementary education. I had secured a teaching job and was excitedly preparing to move to Port Angeles, Washington, to teach 2nd grade. It was a new chapter in my life, and although leaving behind the familiar comfort of my upbringing was daunting, I was eager to embark on this journey. Teaching had always been a passion in my family, passed down from my parents, and I was proud to follow in their footsteps.

Ron and I shared a similar outlook on life, which drew us closer together. His attractive appearance and charming personality further amplified the connection. Ron was unafraid to show his emotions when necessary. You could say he wore his heart on his sleeve. He had a strong presence and was the pillar of strength when it came to making significant decisions in our lives.

That summer became a turning point for both of us. Our decisions were driven by the responsibility of caring for the little human growing inside me. Yes, despite only dating for a couple of months, I found out I was pregnant with Riley.

I carefully considered my options upon discovering my pregnancy. My life had already been planned out, and this unexpected news threw a curveball into everything I had worked towards.

When I shared the news with my parents, I said, "Mom, Dad, I think I'm pregnant."

Mom was in shock. The look on her face said it all. "Here we go again!"

Dad's reaction was a little tense. "I don't believe you. We're going to the drug store to get a pregnancy test," was his retort.

He took me to the uptown drugstore in Butte because we couldn't go to the one by our house. Everyone would know us there, and Dad didn't want to be embarrassed. He bought me two pregnancy tests, took me home, and told me, "I want you to take both tests and let me see the results."

Both tests yielded positive results.

I was already aware of my pregnancy, and there was never any doubt in my mind that I would keep the baby. As a professional with a career, **not** having this child was never an option for me.

Now came the difficult part. Informing my parents had already been a stressful experience. Initially, they were completely shocked, but they eventually warmed up to the idea and provided amazing support. I expected nothing less from these exceptional individuals I am proud to call Mom and Dad.

The ball was now in Ron's court.

Ron traveled to Butte to meet my parents. After the initial introductions, I suggested we take a ride together. It was during this moment that I revealed the news to Ron. I said, "Listen, I'm pregnant! I am going to have this baby. We don't know each other very well, and I will understand if you don't want to be involved in the baby's life. I plan to go to Port Angeles, teach, and raise this child on my own. I will give the baby your last name, and you can come and visit whenever you want. You will be the father with parental rights. I will leave and accept the job, but if you decide you want to play a significant role in this baby's life, you will have to let me know. If we choose to stay together, we will have to get married.

That was my parents' wish, and I told them I would honor it if I decided to stay in Montana. Turns out, Ron's mom had the same thoughts on the matter.

I often wonder, "Why do women feel they must marry the first guy that gets them pregnant?" This is the generation I grew up in and how I was raised. Ron still tells me that fate brought us together. This was in the early 90s, and back then, you got married if you were pregnant. I told Ron, "If you want me to stay, we'll have to get married. It's your choice."

I gave Ron the choice of freedom. It was important to me because we were both involved in this situation, and I didn't want him to feel trapped or excluded from the decision-making process. After all, he would be a father, and that comes with significant responsibilities.

Life presents us with various choices, and I believe these choices shape the person we become. Some individuals opt for the easy way out, making choices that render them weak. Others choose the more challenging path, which doesn't necessarily mean a harder life but often leads to a better one. I didn't want us to feel as though we were ruining our lives. I encouraged Ron to consider his options carefully. We were young and educated, and we would manage either way. However, I didn't want to pressure him. I provided him with an opportunity to opt-out, as often people don't offer that chance and instead resort to ultimatums.

Looking back, I realize how young and irresponsible I was to assume invincibility from SMA or any genetic disease. I wasn't oblivious to the risks, but I allowed myself to be swayed by the impulses and desires of a vulnerable, impressionable 22-year-old. Let alone drag someone else into this mess without giving them a chance to make their own decision. Ron and I shared similar values. We were raised to face challenges head-on, fulfill our responsibilities, and determine what's best for ourselves and everyone involved. We were brought up that you don't shirk your duties. You face these challenges head on. We didn't make decisions lightly. We weighed the pros and cons, seeking a logical solution that would satisfy both parties.

Ron took considerable time to reflect and seek advice from his family and trusted individuals. His careful deliberation demonstrated his strong character and upbringing. He wanted to be a father and actively participate in our baby's life.

When the time came to make his decision, he said, "I want to be part of this baby's life, and we should raise it together. Even though we don't know each other well, I believe we can make it work. Let's give it a try, and then we'll know."

Now I realize that if I had been alone, I can only imagine how things would have turned out raising Riley by myself. Perhaps he wouldn't have received a heart transplant. I am resilient, and I like to think I could have managed, but it would have been much more challenging. Moreover, it would have been unfair to Ron, knowing he had a child but not being involved in every aspect of their upbringing. He didn't want to be a part-time father. We both desired to be a complete family.

When we first got married, our initial connection was rooted more in lust than in love. However, as time passed and we put in the effort, that initial spark transformed into a deep and genuine love. The birth of our children further strengthened our bond, as we both have a strong sense of family values. We consciously decided to prioritize our family and make the most out of challenging circumstances.

Little did we know what lay ahead after Riley was born and diagnosed with *Duchenne muscular dystrophy* (*DMD*). Yet, looking back, if we had never crossed paths, our lives would have taken a completely different trajectory. It feels like fate brought us together for a reason.

Through our journey with Riley and our daughter, Lexi, we have realized that we were meant to raise Riley in this unique way. We were meant to be his advocates, to fight for his life, and to provide him with the best possible childhood and family life alongside his sister Lexi. It's as if this was all part of some Master Plan.

We hold onto hope in the face of adversity. We firmly believe that there is always hope, even in the most demanding situations.

There is HOPE! There is always HOPE!

Chapter 2: Building a Family

Married August 1991

The day I discovered I was pregnant with Riley was a mix of fear and excitement. The circumstances were challenging since Ron and I were not familiar with each other. Altering the course of your life can be traumatic and often lead to disaster. Ron and I had our youth on our side and the passion and compassion to take the plunge. The deck was stacked against us, but we decided to deal with whatever hand we were given and live life to the fullest. With a little human growing inside me, I knew I couldn't raise Riley alone. Ron would be by my side, and we would navigate the road ahead of us together. I would be a mother, he a father, and we would be a family starting a new life together.

Ron and I met in June 1991 and got married on August 29, 1991. Before the wedding, my parents, who were devout Catholics, discussed the appropriate way for me to marry. Since they were going to help us with expenses, we decided to listen. They believed a traditional Catholic wedding in Butte was the right choice. After much thought, they presented us with two options. The first was a grand wedding in the Catholic Church with a reception. The second was a modest ceremony performed by a justice of the peace, followed by a small family gathering. Since this was a much cheaper option, they offered to buy us a new bedroom set and pay off my remaining student loans. After discussing the options with Ron, we decided on the practicality of the second choice.

A Montana Supreme Court Justice officiated our wedding in Helena. It was an intimate ceremony attended by about 20 people at the courthouse. I wore a wedding dress my mother and I had chosen just a week before. Ron was dressed in a blue suit, white shirt, and a red bow tie from his closet. My older sister Maria served as my maid of honor, and Ron's best man was his friend Darren.

We didn't have a professional photographer, so Ron's brother Dan took pictures. After the ceremony, we went to Ron's mom's house and had cake. Later in the evening, we all went to dinner as we were all family now.

That was the day I became Nina Stuart Herrera, Ron's wife. For our honeymoon, Ron and I drove to Calgary, Canada, a five-hour journey from Helena. Since we didn't have much money, we chose to save up for more important things. It provided us with a much-needed break from all the stress we had been experiencing, and it allowed us to focus on being together and getting to know each other before the arrival of our baby.

Some may refer to Ron and me as having had a "shotgun wedding," but here we are, more than 31 years later, still together. We were determined to make our relationship work, unaware that our unborn child would lead us on an incredible journey of self-discovery. Life is truly unpredictable.

Ron would say that our being together was meant to be because FATE made it that way; we found each other. That's why our marriage has lasted for all these years, and we accomplished these miraculous things for Riley.

Bundle of Joy: Riley's Birth

Riley was born on April 11, 1992. My parents were incredibly supportive throughout my pregnancy, but I could sense their worries. I shared their concerns because if our baby were a boy, there was a slight chance he would have *SMA*. A part of me didn't want to know the gender of the baby as it would have added fear to my pregnancy. At the tender age of 22, the last thing I wanted was to dwell on "what-ifs" and potential complications.

We had already chosen names based on the gender. Ron didn't want the baby to be named after him, as he wanted our child to have their own identity. If it were a boy, we settled on the name Riley, which means "Valiant," and suited him perfectly. Moreover, Ron and I met at a restaurant/bar on Canyon Ferry Lake called Riley's, making the name even more fitting. For a girl, we decided on Alexis (Lexi), a name I had always liked.

Starting this new chapter in our lives was undoubtedly stressful. Ron and I didn't have a place of our own. Ron's mom graciously offered us the opportunity to rent the basement in her home for a nominal fee. The basement had a separate entrance through the garage and consisted of a living room, bedroom, and a full bathroom. We set up a small refrigerator and created a makeshift kitchen in part of the living room. We also had a changing table and a bassinet for Riley. Ron was working for the Treasury Department, while I had just secured a part-time job at a daycare to make ends meet. We also had to give up the luxury of having two new cars. Ron had just bought a new Toyota Celica, and I had purchased a new Toyota Tercel. We had both secured great jobs before we met, and purchasing these new vehicles was something we had earned. We took both cars to the dealership several months later and traded them for an older red Ford Escort. It was a far cry from what we had. We knew this was the right choice because we wanted to avoid debt when starting out. The only thing new was the bedroom set my mother and father gave us as a wedding gift.

Aside from all the excitement of pregnancy and the wedding, Ron and I were able to settle into our new normal. We maintained our jobs and lived stable lives. We attended Lamaze classes at our local hospital and went to all our doctor's checkups. I was gaining weight, and the baby was developing normally. Everything was going smoothly during my pregnancy, and nothing out of the ordinary.

The night I delivered Riley was one that I would never forget. It was around 1:30 am, and I felt crampy and uncomfortable. I got up and went to the bathroom, and I remember thinking that I peed a lot. What I didn't know was that my water had broken. I woke Ron up and told him that I was having terrible cramps. We went upstairs to talk to Ron's mom for advice and reassurance that everything was alright. She told us not to worry; we would have plenty of time before the contractions would start, and then we would have to time them.

As we were heading back downstairs, I suddenly experienced an excruciating cramp that stopped me in the middle of the stairs. I had to catch myself and quickly sit down to avoid falling. I looked at Ron with fear and firmly stated, "I don't care what your mom said. I'm going to the hospital right now!"

Ron asked his mom to meet us at the hospital, and he hurriedly got me into the car. By the time we arrived, my contractions were only a minute apart. The nurse informed me that the cramping I had experienced was actual contractions. Ron called my parents to let them know I was at the hospital. We settled into the delivery room at 2:45 am, and that's when I went into labor.

Initially, they didn't want to administer any pain medication because I was managing well, and they anticipated a quick delivery. However, at the last moment, my doctor decided to perform an Episiotomy to prevent tearing due to the rapid delivery.

After receiving a local anesthetic and undergoing the Episiotomy, it was time to start pushing. The doctor used forceps to assist with the delivery and ensure a smooth process. After three intense pushes, our baby boy arrived!!! Ron's mom and my sister, Maria, were there for the birth, and she was overjoyed. It happened so quickly that my parents had not yet arrived at the hospital. They were still making the one-hour trip from Butte. Their amazement was evident when they finally met him upon reaching town.

Riley Gustavo Herrera was born on a beautiful morning at St. Peter's Hospital in Helena, Montana, on April 11, 1992, at 5:25 a.m. He weighed 6 lbs. 13 1/2 oz. and was 20 inches long. Riley received the middle name Gustavo after Ron's father.

When Riley was first born, Ron was so afraid to hold him. He thought he might crush him. Ron carried him on a pillow for the first few weeks of his life. He didn't want anything to happen to him as he cradled him in his arms. I knew right then and there that he would protect Riley no matter what. He loved him so much that I knew we had made the right choice to be together.

I still remember when Riley was so tiny and had his entire life ahead of him. Back then, our thoughts centered on providing him with love and nourishment and ensuring his survival.

We were aware that some people struggle to conceive and would do anything to have a child, regardless of the circumstances. We knew right then that we would do everything in our power to take care of him; after all, raising a child is a privilege. The responsibility of being a parent never fades. As a grown adult, I would still seek advice from my 87-year-old mother. That special bond always remains.

Parents who are trying to conceive yearn for that connection with their child, sometimes to validate their own lives. Their child may face birth complications or have special needs that may only become apparent later in life. Sometimes, a parent may feel that the privilege has become a burden. Life throws us all curveballs, and we must adapt. Riley was never a burden; he was always a source of joy.

We often look down on or look differently at things that are foreign or unknown to us. It's like peeling the layers of an onion: There's always one more layer to understand. We all wear different hats when bringing a child into our lives. We need to show empathy and understanding for all parents and the troubles they may be going through.

The birth of Riley was one of the most joyous moments in my life. Ron and I embraced parenthood and gradually adjusted to our new roles. One month after Riley's arrival, we moved out of Ron's mother's house to begin our independent life. Inge, Ron's mom, had been incredibly generous, and it was bittersweet for her to see us leave. However, she understood the importance of us standing on our own two feet.

Ron's position at work was initially part-time, but soon, he left for training as a special agent. His training was scheduled to take place in Glynco, GA, at the *Federal Law Enforcement Training Center* (*FLETC*), and he would be away for a period of six months. We decided that I would take our son, Riley, and go live with my parents in Butte, MT. They were able to provide the support I needed, and they were thrilled to have their grandson with them. Living with my parents during those six months was a wonderful experience. I needed to find employment, and my mom helped me secure a job at the YMCA daycare. My parents pitched in to help care for Riley while I went to work. They also provided financial support by covering all my expenses. This arrangement was incredibly beneficial for Ron and me as we were able to save every penny we earned.

When Ron completed his training and returned home, we moved back to Helena, MT, while he waited for news about his transfer to start his new job as a Special Agent. We felt it was the right moment to have Riley baptized during this time. Religion played a significant role in our upbringing, as we were raised Catholic. I held strong convictions about this matter, and since we were living in Helena and Ron had attended St. Cyril and Methodius in East Helena, MT, we decided to have Riley baptized there.

The next step was choosing godparents; I couldn't choose just one. I wanted all three of my brothers to be Riley's godfathers because they had played such important roles in my life. Although conventionally, you're supposed to choose only one godfather, I couldn't imagine leaving any of them out. I remember sharing the news with my brothers, and they were ecstatic. Even though they couldn't attend the wedding due to their recent move to Las Vegas, NV, they weren't going to miss out on Riley's baptism. They were overjoyed at the opportunity to be bestowed with the title of godfather.

As for the godmother, I selected my sister, Maria, who had served as my Maid of Honor. She also cared for me when I was younger, so it felt right to include her. Ron also wanted a family member to be a godparent, so he chose his sister Lisa to be Riley's co-godmother. Riley's baptism took place on January 3, 1993, and our future looked incredibly promising.

Shortly after, Ron's job opportunity opened in Billings, Montana. We packed up Riley and our modest belongings to move, allowing Ron to embark on his new career. We rented a small unit above a garage, with our landlords residing in the main house. It was the beginning of our journey as we started carving out our little space in the world.

Riley's development progressed normally during those crucial months. He achieved the milestone of sitting up unsupported at six months and began uttering "Da, Da" and "Ma, Ma." At seven and a half months, he started scooting, and two months later, he began crawling. We were thrilled when Riley took his first steps on May 16, 1993, at 13 months old. It happened on a Sunday, and he managed to take ten steps! Ron and I were elated as Riley exceeded our expectations and met all the developmental milestones for his age. As a new mom and not knowing what the future may bring, I was particularly attentive and watchful, anticipating any challenges that may come our way.

Began Noticing Muscle Weakness

I could tell that something was happening physically to Riley at a very young age. It was a traumatic realization, and at the time, I was only 24 years old. I pushed it to the back of my mind, refusing to accept it as truth. I kept my concerns hidden, never sharing them with anyone. Growing up with two brothers with *Spinal muscular atrophy (SMA)* gave me an acute eye for recognizing such signs.

The first time I noticed that something wasn't right was when Riley was 17 months old. It was only four months after he had taken his first steps, but on that day, something clicked for me. We were at a wedding at the Cathedral in Helena, Montana, and all the children were playing on the steps. I observed that Riley couldn't jump as high or walk as fast as the other kids. I was accustomed to working with preschool children and was attuned to these differences.

Psychologically, I wasn't ready to deal with something this severe, and I wanted to protect everyone. I always had that DAMN monkey on my back. Looking back, I wonder how I was able to handle all of this. I kept it to myself to protect the people I love. It was an onerous burden to carry, but it was one that I was willing to take on.

Another Joyful Arrival

We were excited about starting our life in Billings and being independent. Ron was embarking on a new career, and I had secured a teaching job at a preschool in Laurel, MT, just outside Billings. The town was a short 15-minute commute from Billings, and Riley attended daycare there while I worked. We were utilizing our education, and all seemed to be right with the world.

The news of my second pregnancy brought immense joy to Ron and me. Although having more children had been a topic of discussion, this pregnancy was also a surprise to us. Riley continued to reach milestones and progress to the naked eye, even fooling Ron.

Our families shared in our happiness upon learning the exciting news. Since we still lived in Billings, I called my parents to share the update. I could sense my mother's hesitation in her voice as I told her about the pregnancy. While she was happy for Ron and me, she couldn't help but worry if it was the right decision. She always had our best interests at heart, having endured her fair share of struggles while raising us. My father, as usual, was a man of few words. His voice carried a hint of tension as if saying, "Here we go again!"

I embarked on the journey of bringing another new life into this world and made it my priority to ensure a smooth and effortless pregnancy. Despite the barriers, I remained focused on providing the necessary care for Riley. I dedicated myself to meeting his needs and ensuring his well-being alongside the demands of pregnancy.

The next nine months flew right by. When I felt my first contraction this time, I knew exactly what it was. I contacted our doctor to inform him of my contractions, and he advised us to come to the hospital immediately. He knew my history and how quickly Riley had arrived in the world. We arrived at St. Vincent Hospital in Billings at 8:00 am. At 10:15 am, on June 12, 1994, Alexis Mary Herrera was born, weighing six pounds and a half ounce and measuring 20 inches in length. We chose the middle name Mary in honor of my mother.

With the arrival of Lexi, our family felt complete. We became a united force, the Four Musketeers. Riley was just 26 months old when his sister arrived. Having a son and a daughter has brought us unexplicable joy. Moreover, Lexi became the beacon of light we desperately needed. During my pregnancy with her, I was filled with nerves, and it was then that I began noticing Riley's physical difficulties.

Being a parent to both a son and a daughter has been a remarkable and fulfilling experience. However, Riley's birth accompanied an additional layer of emotions. I felt an immense sense of relief, knowing that she had a significantly lower risk of developing *Spinal muscular atrophy* (*SMA*). This relief stemmed from the fact that *SMA* is more commonly found in boys, and having a daughter meant that she had a better chance of not inheriting this condition.

Riley & Lexi

Throughout this journey, I embraced a forward-looking mindset, refusing to dwell on the past and instead living fully in the present. Each day became an opportunity to embrace and cherish, eagerly anticipating what the future holds. I firmly believe our future lies in the days ahead, not the distant weeks, months, and years. This perspective has been our guiding light throughout the years.

In the face of any difficulties or uncertainties, I hold onto one constant: hope. Hope has become a constant companion, reminding me that there is always a glimmer of possibility, even in the darkest moments. It is hope that fuels my resilience and keeps me moving forward, confident that brighter days will come.

So, as I traverse the joys and challenges of motherhood and build a future for my children, I hold onto hope with steadfast faith. Hope is a powerful force that propels us forward, illuminating the path ahead.

There is HOPE! There is always HOPE!

Dianne DeMille, Ph.D. and Nina Stuart Herrera

Chapter 3: Duchenne Muscular Dystrophy

What is Duchenne Muscular Dystrophy?

Duchenne muscular dystrophy (*DMD*) is a rare disease caused by a genetic mutation that prevents the body from producing dystrophin protein. Dystrophin is needed for the muscles in our body to work correctly. Without it, muscle cells become fragile to the point of cardiac failure.

Most women affected by a genetic mutation that can cause Duchenne will not develop the disease. However, they can pass the mutation on to a son who will have *Duchenne* or to a daughter who will become a "carrier" of the mutation like her mother.

Some women carriers of a *Duchenne* mutation may eventually develop signs or symptoms, which are usually far more subtle than actual *DMD*. But it's also possible for girls or women with this kind of mutation to develop more involved symptoms, including *Duchenne*, the same as in boys and men. Cases of females with *DMD* are rare.

The leading cause of death with *DMD* is cardio-respiratory failure. Children with *DMD* have problems breathing and walking because of the damaged muscle development in these areas. The heart muscle may fail. It is a progressive and irreversible disease, and currently, there is no cure.

The life span of children born with *Duchenne muscular dystrophy* (*DMD*) has increased. It is now possible for people with *DMD* to survive into their early thirties. Some cases now report men living into their forties and fifties. Many are now able to attend college and have careers. Some are even able to get married and have children. *Duchenne* is carried on the X chromosome. A man with *DMD* cannot pass the flawed gene to his son because he gives a son a Y chromosome, not an X. But he will pass it to his daughters because each daughter inherits her father's only X chromosome.

Becker MD and *Duchenne MD* are similar; however, *Becker* is much less severe. It was something many said Riley had when he was first diagnosed. *Duchenne* occurs in one in 3,500- 5,000 boys worldwide and 400-600 in the United States. The average age for diagnosis is five, with more than 90% in wheelchairs by age 15.[1]

Riley Diagnosis: Age Four

Even before Riley was diagnosed, my mom and brothers suspected something was wrong, but they never told me because they didn't want to scare me. Little did they know I had the same suspicions.

Greg continued, "We would watch Riley when he was young, and we started noticing little things. We could see that little glitch he had when he walked. We became experts in the field at seeing these things. Mom also wondered if we noticed the same things, 'Do you think there's something wrong with him? How he's getting up, he walks like a bear.'"

I responded, "During that time, Ron and I were trying to figure things out. We didn't have a clue because we thought he must have *SMA*. What did you guys think? Did Mom think he had *SMA*?"

"What else could you think?" replied Dave.

Greg said, "No, I didn't! I didn't say it, but I thought he had *DMD*. That doctor was probably right. Like me, he had early signs when he was a child, and I was not surprised."

Friday, March 24, 1995, is a day that will forever be etched in my memory, although I desperately wish I could forget it. It was a day when my world collapsed, leaving me breathless and overwhelmed with sorrow. Even as I write these words, a lump forms in my throat, and tears well up in my eyes.

This fateful day occurred just two days after my 25th birthday when we visited Riley's pediatrician in Billings, Montana. As he examined Riley, I watched anxiously, hoping for reassuring words. However, the doctor's expression grew grave, and he asked Riley to perform various tasks, such as walking and running. After conducting some strength tests, he turned to me and said, "Nina, I believe there's something wrong with Riley. I think you should take him to a neurologist. I'm not entirely certain of the exact condition, but there are some concerns."

My heart sank as he described what he had observed. "I notice the way he's getting up and walking is not what I'd like to see. He is walking with a waddling gait and on his toes. Riley also has hypertrophy in his

36

calves; it makes them look muscular, but they are not. He is expressing signs of *muscular dystrophy*."

It was a devastating blow, and I collapsed to my knees, feeling the blood drain from my face. It was a gut punch as if everything I had noticed since Riley was 17 months old had finally come to fruition.

The memories of that day send shivers down my spine. It was my worst nightmare come true, a pain no parent should ever have to experience. I had to gather my strength for Riley's sake, concealing my inner turmoil so as not to upset him. I had to be strong and not let him know how upset I was. I was able to maintain my composure until we returned home, where I could finally let my emotions flow.

I knew I had to share the news with Ron, but the thought of burdening him with this life-altering information was unbearable. Breaking the news to him was one of the most agonizing tasks I have ever faced. We were devastated, but Ron, in his gentle and kind manner, suggested we follow the pediatrician's advice and seek a definitive diagnosis for Riley. "We need to know for certain what Riley is facing," he said.

Following our pediatrician's recommendation, we arranged blood work to test Riley's *creatine phosphokinase* (*CPK*) levels, indicating muscle damage. *Creatine phosphokinase* is an intracellular muscle enzyme involved in energy metabolism. It is released into the bloodstream when muscle cells break down. The levels are significantly elevated in dystrophic diseases, reflecting muscle breakdown. This simple test would provide valuable information for the neurologist.

The results revealed that Riley's *CPK* levels were around 14,000, while the average level was around 100. The doctors explained that such levels indicated severe muscle trauma and damage, akin to the aftermath of a major car accident. That was the reality of Riley's body. We didn't fully comprehend the significance at the time, but we now know that those levels pointed towards *Duchenne muscular dystrophy* (*DMD*). Interestingly, we later found out that my brothers Greg and Dave had *CPK* levels within the normal range.

As I settled Riley into his car seat for the appointment with the Neurologist, tears streamed down my face. The weight of the situation overwhelmed me. Riley has always been our motivation, our driving force to confront challenges head-on. How could this innocent child be subjected to such a traumatic ordeal? I have already lived through this with my brothers. And now I must relive everything AGAIN! I felt an unimaginable sense of déjà vu.

When we finally visited the neurologist, her demeanor was initially curt and tense, creating an atmosphere of unease. She barked orders at Riley like a drill sergeant while conducting muscle tests, instructing him to lie on the floor, get up, walk down the hall, and run back to us. Riley performed these tasks to the best of his ability, and that seemed to be all she needed to see. Without any consideration for our emotions, she bluntly declared, "I believe he has *Duchenne muscular dystrophy*. You'll need further testing to confirm this, but he will most likely require a wheelchair by the age of 10 and be dead by 17. You need to go home and learn to accept it."

Her words struck us like a sharp blow, and I had to resist the urge to lash out in anger. I wanted to reach out and smack her. Her bedside manner was appalling, lacking any empathy or sensitivity. How could she deliver such devastating news in such a cold and matter-of-fact manner? Have some couth! It felt like a cruel and heartless death sentence. Did she expect us to surrender to despair? Hearing such hurtful words at such a vulnerable moment was unimaginably painful for any parent. She didn't even attempt to soften the blow.

A quote about "FEAR has two meanings: 1) Forget Everything and Run. OR 2) Face Everything and Rise. The choice is yours."[2]

"We chose to face everything and rise," a powerful quote that encapsulates our determination in the face of adversity.

I told her, "This is unacceptable. You don't know us."

Ron piped in, "You don't know Riley or what we will go through for him. You can't tell us he is going to die!" He expressed his disbelief at her assertion. The intensity in his voice meant that he was up for a fight.

That was the first and last time we ever saw that doctor. Even now, I remain infuriated and flabbergasted by her insensitive delivery of such life-altering news. I can't help but wonder how many other families she brought to their knees with her callousness.

The weight of the situation immediately settled in my mind, and thoughts of my family flooded in. How could this be? Riley with *DMD*, and Greg and Dave with *SMA*? Maybe Greg and Dave were misdiagnosed, or maybe she was wrong about Riley. How could I possibly convey such devastating news over the phone? It all felt so surreal, like a nightmare I couldn't wake up from.

Our Support Team

That night, Ron and I sat down to discuss how we would handle the situation regarding Riley's health. Ron took the initiative to research and find the best doctor who could conduct the necessary testing for Riley. It was crucial for us to obtain a definite diagnosis. I remember telling Ron that Riley had to have *SMA*. I said, "I know how this will progress; if Riley is showing signs of *SMA* at an early age, he is just like Greg." Greg was in a wheelchair by age 18.

But before I could inform Mom and Dad, I needed to speak with Greg and Dave first. They had experienced this type of news before and could offer guidance on how to process it. They might also offer some insight and advice on how we could break the news to our parents.

I first called Greg and Dave and told them about Riley. They couldn't believe it. Dave said, "What is going on here? Is our family cursed?"

I vividly remember recounting to Greg and Dave the exact words the neurologist spoke. She suspected that Riley had *Duchenne muscular dystrophy* (*DMD*).

Dave remembers when I said, "'The doctor says Riley has a general weakness.' I knew right away that it was some form of what we have because of our family's history."

I explained to Greg and Dave that although both conditions fall under the umbrella of *muscular dystrophy*, the neurologist specifically believed Riley had *Duchenne muscular dystrophy*, which set his diagnosis apart from theirs. It was just so disheartening for them to hear this news. They knew *DMD* was a much more sinister disease than *SMA*.

We knew our parents planned to visit Greg, Dave, and Chris in Las Vegas in the coming days. They intended to offer support as Dave had recently suffered a broken tibia and fibula when his leg got caught under a kitchen cabinet.

We all decided not to inform them immediately, as we didn't want them to receive such distressing news until they were with my brothers in Vegas. I remember my voice cracking when I told them, "I don't want to tell Mom and Dad right now. It will be too much for them to bear by themselves."

After waiting for our parents to settle in Las Vegas, Greg and Dave revealed the news to them. Dave recalls informing them, "The doctor thinks Riley has some general weakness. He has some delayed development and difficulty getting up."

Greg added, "As soon as you said, 'general weakness,' Mom knew, and she started crying and fell apart. She didn't want to talk to anyone. She was unable to hold herself together. She was devastated and didn't want to interact with anyone."

Dave also remembers her words, "Mom said, 'I can't believe this is happening to our family. We already have two people in the family. We're reliving it again!'"

Greg added, "I remember how upset she was, and I know Dad didn't want to say anything either. Dad never said much. He was a quiet man. Mom said, 'I don't want to listen to this!' She was in shock and experienced a mental breakdown."

Mom had to be prescribed medication to help her cope with the news about Riley. The medication provided some relief as they had to focus on taking care of Dave and his injured leg. This eased the burden on Mom's mind, as she wasn't constantly consumed by thoughts of Riley. The situation was devastating for them. It was unimaginable, reliving the

Frustrated, Greg firmly asserted, "No, we're not connected! I never tested positive for *Becker*, not even at the *University of Utah* when I was six. They performed a biopsy, and the results were negative. I went to the *Mayo Clinic*, and they confirmed it. It's *Spinal muscular atrophy* (SMA). It's not *Duchenne* or *Becker muscular dystrophy*."

At that moment, I realized we were grasping at straws here. The disbelief surrounding our situation was overwhelming. We appreciated that *Denver Children's Hospital* initiated the genetic journey for our family. However, we all knew we needed more concrete proof to determine the exact nature of Riley's condition and to provide a correct diagnosis for my brothers. Additional testing would be required to distinguish between *Duchenne* and *Becker muscular dystrophy* for Riley and to clarify the diagnoses of Greg and Dave. *Denver Children's Hospital* could only take us so far. Our next step was in Dr. Eric Hoffman and his team's capable hands.

Finding the Right Answers

Doctor Hoffman's resume was impressive. He was a Professor and Associate Dean at *Binghamton University*, "assistant professor of neurology at Harvard Medical School and Children's Hospital Boston, professor of molecular genetics and biochemistry at the University of Pittsburgh School of Medicine, director of the Center for Genetic Medicine at the Children's National Medical Center, and professor and chair of the Department of Integrative Systems Biology at George Washington University. His research has focused on the genetic basis of human and animal disease, drug development and genetic variation in human populations."[3]

He has done clinical trials and drug development in *Duchenne muscular dystrophy* (*DMD*) and other neuromuscular disorders. He was one of the research doctors who helped identify the *DMD dystrophin* gene, which codes for a protein called dystrophin. A gene mutation here will result in a loss of the dystrophin protein, leading to the degeneration of muscle fibers.

Receiving the news that Dr. Hoffman had received a portion of Riley's muscle biopsy, paperwork, and blood samples, along with those of my brothers, was a significant moment. It meant that all our information was in the hands of an expert who could provide us with some much-needed answers. The long wait finally came to an end in 1997 when, after two years of testing, we received a conclusive diagnosis for Riley. The tests revealed that Riley had less than 3% dystrophin, officially confirming his diagnosis of *Duchenne muscular dystrophy* (*DMD*).

The tests also confirmed what doctors at the *Mayo Clinic* had suspected all those years ago. Greg and Dave had *Spinal muscular atrophy* (*SMA*). It was a validation of their expertise and a confirmation that their initial diagnosis was correct.

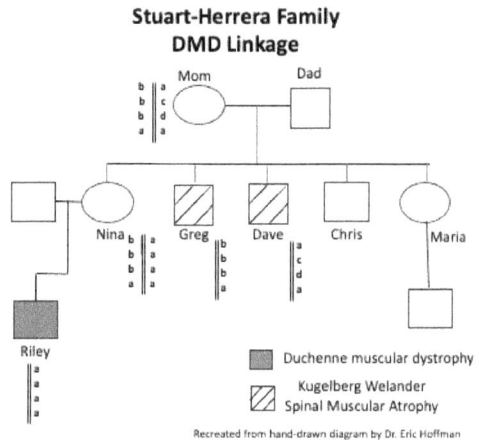

Stuart-Herrera Family DMD Linkage

Recreated from hand-drawn diagram by Dr. Eric Hoffman

Greg added, "Dr. Hoffman at the *University of Pittsburgh* could see on the chromosomes that Dave and I have *SMA*. It sticks out like a sore thumb."

Dr. Eric Hoffman said, "There's no question that Dave and Greg have *SMA*, and Riley has *DMD*."[4]

The SMN1 gene responsible for causing Spinal muscular atrophy was discovered in 1995.[5]

Following Riley's diagnosis, we decided to conduct linkage studies within our family. It was important to determine if Lexi, our daughter, was a carrier for *SMA* or *DMD*. We sent her blood work and lab reports to Baylor College of Medicine for extensive linkage studies. The initial results indicated Lexi was "unlikely" to carry the *DMD* gene because she did not inherit the same allele, an alternative form of a specific gene, as Riley. We felt a sense of relief, thinking that we were in the clear. That relief was short-lived. It turned out that Lexi does carry the gene for *SMA*. This unexpected twist left us astounded.

I remember one of the doctors telling us, "Sorry, but you guys just have bad luck."

Other doctors have also told us that the chances of us having two types of *muscular dystrophy* in our family are "one in a million." Why can't we just hit the lottery instead?

They were able to confirm that Lexi carries *SMA* but not *DMD*. We thought the gene had mutated, and we talked about it. They told us, "No, a third of the people who have a child with *Duchenne* is spontaneous, and it happens at conception, and that's what happened to you."

I was never a carrier of *DMD*. It was unimaginable to think, "How can we have two *muscular dystrophy* diseases in the family, with two of my brothers and then my son?"

Greg said, "Nobody knows who the carrier for *SMA* was before Mom or Dad. We had our blood tested, and they estimated a 99.4% chance our parents were both carriers of *SMA*."

No one anticipates being thrust into a life like ours. Ron was caught off guard by the challenges that came our way. He has always been a determined and driven individual. The nature of this work requires a person with strong nerves, and I am grateful to have Ron by my side. Without him, I would not have been able to do it alone.

Dave recounted a conversation in which Ron said, "I hope that Riley turns out like you." It struck a chord with Dave because, for many years, he walked. Ron's wish was for Riley to be able to walk like him rather than face the serious limitations imposed by DMD.

Ron's famous saying is, "I want my kid to be like his Uncle Buddy." Dave's nickname as he is affectionately known by all his nephews and nieces.

To hear Dave recall that still cuts like a knife. Talk about picking the lesser of two evils.

Greg shared his admiration for Ron, acknowledging that he fought harder for Riley than anyone else because he saw the potential and refused to accept the situation. "While some people might question what they had gotten themselves into, Ron never wavered. He wholeheartedly embraced the role of a devoted parent and took it on. His unwavering commitment and determination have always earned my respect. Ron could have easily chosen to walk away, but he chose to put Riley first, regardless of the difficulties they faced."

Dave added, "Men often struggle to cope with situations like these and may choose to leave. However, Ron stayed, demonstrating his strength and dedication."

Dave revealed that our father rarely discussed such issues, but Mom was always inquiring. Riley held a unique place in my dad's heart because he grew up with two sons with *SMA* and now had a grandson facing a similar challenge. Although he never explicitly said it, Riley's situation resonated with him deeply.

Greg told me that Ron and I had done everything right when it came to Riley. He believed that Riley's life could have been in jeopardy without our efforts. Dave also echoed this sentiment, emphasizing his enduring respect for Ron.

Dave said, " We've been told many things about our disease growing up. We always kept an eye on how Riley was doing for every little thing. We looked at Lexi, too. Robert was much earlier, but he was fine. He was healthy. "

"I'm 61 now. I'm not complaining," added Greg.

Dave further stated, "I've done well. I've had a lot of ups and downs, and we've been through a lot. Hey, I'm 58 years old. They told me I wouldn't live past 18 or 20."

Greg told Dave, "We had each other and never accepted that diagnosis."

Dave said, "We're going to keep on living and let the chips fall where they may. *Muscular Dystrophy Association* would call us and say some treatment might be coming. I would tell them, 'Okay, call me when you find a cure!' That's what Riley does. He lives his own life. He's an amazing human being and one of the most courageous people I've ever met."

It's important to note that my brother's *SMA* and Riley's *DMD* are unrelated. They are on completely different genes. They exist side by side but do not intersect. Having both diseases within our family is truly remarkable, and moving forward was our only option.

The diagnosis for Riley was incredibly difficult to accept. Looking back at what my brothers endured, I wouldn't wish these diseases upon my worst enemy. It was a profound learning experience for all of us, and we knew our lives would never be the same.

I found myself questioning, "Now that we have this, where do we go from here?" As parents, we had to summon immense willpower, strength, empathy, and compassion to ensure our son's survival in the face of this devastating disease. Our youth worked to our advantage, as fearlessness pushed us to confront and make the best of our situation. We made countless calls, sought medical care, and did everything necessary for Riley's well-being. I often wonder if I would still possess that same mental state now; as we grow older, we tend to overthink things.

Ron actively researched *DMD*, seeking knowledge about the disease and how to navigate everyday life with it. Meanwhile, my focus was on caregiving and ensuring Riley and Lexi had everything they needed.

Happiness is not a destination; it encompasses everything in between and celebrates the little moments. It's a roller coaster ride we experience every day. Our challenge has been finding a balance in our everyday life, ensuring that both Riley and Lexi feel equally important. Except for my family, we've always had a different definition of "normal" than those around us.

When we received Riley's diagnosis, we decided to provide him with the comprehensive care he needed. We believed in treating his entire body, incorporating both Eastern and Western medicine and philosophies. We explored various natural and homeopathic remedies, including bee pollen and a friend's recommendation of a particular type of water with osmosis. If it didn't interfere with his regular medications or cause harm, we were willing to try anything.

Knowing that the progression of Riley's disease would limit our ability to travel in the future, we were determined to give him as many experiences as possible while he was still able. When our children were younger, we embarked on numerous vacations, exploring different parts of the United States and even visiting several other countries.

I had complete faith in our family and the doctors who cared for Riley. I believed that we would overcome this as a family, that Riley would overcome his challenges, that Ron would provide the support we needed, and that Lexi would come to terms with the situation as well. Riley became our priority not because he was loved more but because he faced the most difficulties.

Ron and I were determined there was no way Riley would not go to school or college. We never thought he wouldn't do it. We didn't know how, but we would make sure he had ordinary experiences, and sometimes, normal can be challenging. Having a terminal disease is not normal.

Ron coined the nickname "The Beast" for *Duchenne muscular dystrophy* because just when we thought we had control, "The Beast" would rear its ugly head with a new set of daunting and difficult challenges.

In March of 2000, Dr. Hoffman's lab had Riley's gene sequenced, and we discovered he had a duplication of exon two on the gene. The gene is made up of 79 exons. Ron explains that these 79 exons are like a recipe to build protein. Because Riley has a duplication of exon 2, the protein recipe must be fixed early in the process. In recent years, scientists have devised a way to "skip" specific exons on the gene. He may have a more normal protein if they can skip over his duplicated exon 2. This type of therapy may prolong his life by stopping the progression of the disease.

From my perspective, these experiences have been a rollercoaster of emotions. They have involved seeking answers, receiving diagnoses, and encountering unexpected findings. This underscores the importance of relying on expert medical opinions and the need for accurate and thorough testing to understand and manage these medical conditions.

Armed with this newfound knowledge about Riley's disease, we gained hope. Hope that we can find a treatment until a cure is discovered and faith that Riley can live a long and fulfilling life.

Duchenne muscular dystrophy affects boys differently depending on the location of the flaw on the large gene. Some boys are born with mental disabilities and experience developmental or physical limitations. By the age of four or five, some are confined to wheelchairs, while others may have little to no brain function or the ability to feed themselves. Riley was lucky to be able to do the many things he has achieved.[6]

I cannot express enough gratitude for the tireless efforts of Dr. Eric Hoffman and his colleagues, who have supported us throughout this journey. These tireless professionals have dedicated their entire lives to diagnosing, treating, managing, and curing our children. Without them, we would be completely lost. They are a shining light in the darkness that surrounds us.

There is HOPE! There is always HOPE!

Dianne DeMille, Ph.D. and Nina Stuart Herrera

Chapter 4: Living with DMD

Beginning to Live with DMD as a family

We adapted and got into the routine of raising Riley and Lexi. Our little apartment had a large backyard with a swing set. The kids absolutely loved it. Eventually, we purchased a split-level home and settled into a quiet neighborhood. We were beginning to experience the joys of parenthood.

After living in Billings, Montana, for about two years, Ron received an unexpected opportunity to move back to Helena, his hometown. There was an opening in his department that he couldn't resist. Once again, our lives were upended.

Fortunately, this move proved to be beneficial for Ron's career and our family. It meant that I would be closer to my family in Butte, Montana, while Ron had most of his family, including his mother, in Helena. We decided to take a leap of faith. Little did we know, my brothers Greg and Dave had also made the decision to move back to Montana. When we heard the news of their move, we were overjoyed. It meant they would be closer to us and could offer support whenever needed. It seemed like fate was bringing us together to face whatever challenges lay ahead.

Our move to Helena was filled with both excitement and anxiety. We were thrilled to return to Ron's hometown, but at the same time, we were apprehensive about the uncertainties surrounding Riley's condition. Our first task was to find a new house where we could begin the next chapter of our lives. After careful consideration, Ron and I settled on a wonderful home in the Helena Valley. The neighborhood was welcoming and filled with children around Riley and Lexi's ages, and the school district had an excellent reputation. We knew we had made the right choice.

Nightly Ritual

And He will raise you up on eagles' wings.
Bear you on the breath of dawn.
Make you shine like the sun.

And hold you in the palm of His hand.[7]

During my upbringing, this song was one of my mom's favorites, which we often sang at church. Its lyrics would come to mind during difficult times, offering solace and reminding me that I was not alone. Being back in Helena felt like a blessing. We moved into our new home, excited for a fresh start. Our faith played a significant role in guiding our decisions during Riley's and Lexi's formative years. We held onto the hope that we could face any challenge together. Personally, I strongly

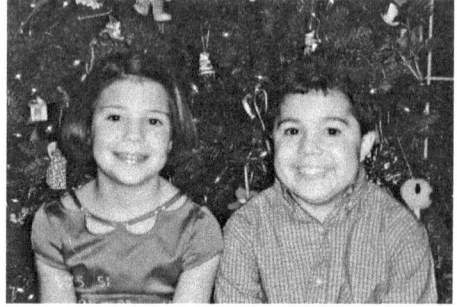

Lexi & Riley

believe in the power of prayer. Growing up Catholic, prayer had always been a part of my life, both in times of joy and in times of hardship.

Ron, too, believed in the power of prayer for the well-being of our family. In moments of crisis, he would often turn to prayer for comfort. A nightly ritual was established, where Ron would kneel by Riley and Lexi's bedside and offer his prayers. It was time for reflection, helping him steer our path with Riley. Afterward, he would kneel by our own bedside, silently praying. As I watched him with love and admiration, I pondered the content of his prayers and the words he silently recited in his mind. But I knew, deep down, that we were praying for the same thing.

There were moments when I felt overwhelmed, carrying the world's weight on my shoulders and becoming disillusioned. During those times, Ron would step in with his unwavering faith. He always believed in God. While he was baptized as a Catholic, he wasn't raised with the same level of religious involvement as I was. Ron believed that being a devout Catholic didn't necessarily require attending church every Sunday. He believed that true faith resided within a person and that practicing Catholicism meant living out your faith wherever you were, not just within the walls of a church. He often reminded me that God didn't hide in the corner of a church, ensuring that we attended mass. God already knew if we believed in Him, and that was what mattered.

During that time, we took Riley to Denver to begin his diagnosis of *Duchenne muscular dystrophy (DMD)*. My brothers relocated back to our area and considered moving to Helena to be closer to us. After the dust settled, they ended up moving to Great Falls, Montana, where they quickly found suitable housing. We were thrilled because it was only 83 miles away from us.

Ron's job transfer went smoother than expected, and we began our new chapter in Helena. Despite everything we were about to go through, Riley and Lexi were adjusting remarkably well.

Kids can be incredibly resilient, unlike some adults, who become more cynical with age. Life experiences can shape us that way. Ron and I always tried to see things through Riley's eyes. He had a unique way of looking at life through rose-colored glasses and always strived to make the best out of a bad situation. Even when he was at his lowest point, he showed compassion for others and reminded us that people out there had it worse than him. He taught us humility, and we like to think that Ron and I had a hand in that.

Amidst the chaos of medical appointments, we still had to carry on with our lives. Ron and I firmly believed in maintaining as much normalcy as possible. Our children needed us to stay present, and we needed to present a united front. After we moved, I made the decision to stay at home with Riley and Lexi to help them adjust to the new home and neighborhood. I always felt anxious during significant life events because I wanted a smooth transition for Riley. However, I managed to find an excellent preschool for him, Early Movement Preschool in Helena. It was owned and operated by someone originally from Butte, and it turned out to be a perfect fit for Riley. He thoroughly enjoyed every moment he spent there. Despite Riley's *muscular dystrophy* not being easily recognizable at that point, I did inform the school about his situation, and they were incredibly accepting. None of the parents asked questions, and I didn't offer any additional information since we were still in the dark about his diagnosis. Riley could still run, jump to some extent, and get up from the floor without any difficulty. This was his time to experience life as a typical child.

Riley became good friends with another boy at preschool, and I struck up a friendship with his mother. The boys started having playdates, and Riley once again got to experience the joys of a regular childhood. The boy's parents were a nurse and a doctor, respectively, and when I explained Riley's situation, they were more than accepting and understanding. They assured me that if anything happened, they would contact us. Why not let the kids be kids? They had two boys, and sometimes Lexi would tag along on the playdates as well.

Riley didn't want to come home on one particular playdate, so my friend asked if he could stay the night. I trusted these parents completely and knew that Riley would be safe with them. I remember discussing the sleepover with another mom who was taken aback and said, "Oh my God, you let your preschooler sleep over at someone's house?" Yes, we were living in the present, not knowing what tomorrow might bring. It was wonderful to have that kind of relationship and to surround ourselves with like-minded people who allowed the children to have fun. The kids needed those experiences, and we had built a trusting relationship with this family. The kids eagerly looked forward to many more good times. You never know when there might come a time when all that might end.

Sometimes, I felt like a fish out of water because we didn't know anyone else who had a child with *DMD*. I was unsure how much to disclose about Riley's condition, fearing he might be ostracized if other parents didn't want their children to associate with him. But then, I would remember the values my parents instilled in all of us: to live life as normally as possible and surround ourselves with good people. Most importantly, we were taught to keep moving forward and focus on the future rather than dwelling on what could have been. We concentrated on the road ahead and embraced every situation as a teachable moment, whether it was good or bad. Never stop learning!

Dealing with Adversity

It doesn't matter who you are; your life will always have pitfalls. How you handle them can make you stronger or send you spiraling in the other direction. We always tried to lift ourselves by our bootstraps and gave it our best shot.

We have all experienced prejudice or discrimination at least once, and these instances often have a profound impact on our lives. They teach us how to face adversity, shape our character, and help us discover who we aspire to be.

I want to share a few encounters involving Riley that significantly influenced our personal growth. Prejudice and discrimination can manifest in various forms, such as bullying, racial discrimination, or simply a lack of understanding and empathy. The following examples have remained vivid in my memory and continue to resonate with me to this day.

I distinctly recall an incident at the supermarket when Riley accompanied me. Life was inspiring and exhausting as a young mother with a newborn. In my rush to get to the grocery store, I didn't have time to shower or fix myself up. I threw my hair into a ponytail and wore sweats without any makeup. With Riley by my side, we embarked on our errand. I noticed a few glances directed at us, assuming they were either admiring the baby or perhaps noticing my disheveled appearance.

However, my assumptions were challenged when an elderly woman approached me in the middle of an aisle. She complimented Riley, remarking on his beauty. I responded affirmatively and mentioned that his father was of Latin American descent. To my surprise, she questioned who I was babysitting for. I clarified that I was Riley's mother. Despite her evident shock, she commented on my young age and expressed disbelief that he didn't resemble me. I informed her of my age, reiterated that I was Riley's mother, and walked away.

A similar experience occurred when I reached the checkout line. Once again, I had to remind someone of my identity and how I fit into Riley's life. Such insensitivity can be disheartening.

These encounters profoundly impacted my perspective on how I presented myself going forward. From then on, I made conscious efforts to leave the house looking presentable. I also resolved not to be the shy, uncertain young mother anymore. Instead, I chose to be assertive and confident, proud of being a mother, and unashamed of bringing Riley into this world. When faced with the same inquiries about Lexi, if someone questioned their relationship with me, I would confidently assert that I am her mother. This change in attitude has served me well throughout my life, teaching me the importance of standing up for myself.

While I understand that these questions were not intended to cause harm, they sometimes made me feel invisible. It wasn't until another incident in our neighborhood that I recognized these instances as prejudice and discrimination.

"Ignorance breeds fear and hatred," is a quote by Kristin Cast.[8] This quote resonates with a situation my children encountered at a very young age. It's not something I like to dwell on, but it's crucial to understand Riley's story. No parent or child should ever feel inferior due to the color of their skin or a disability they may have. I have strived to raise my children with tolerance and the ability to see things from multiple perspectives.

Growing up in a small town in Montana, my parents instilled in me the value of giving everyone a second chance, sometimes even three or four, depending on the circumstances. However, due to the demographics of our area, there was limited exposure to racial and ethnic diversity. Montana's population predominantly consists of white individuals, as indicated by a recent *March of Dimes* poll conducted in 2020 that revealed approximately 85.7% of Montana's population identified as white, while American Indian/Alaska Native individuals accounted for 6.0%, Hispanics accounted for 4.2%, Asian/Pacific Islanders accounted for 1.0%, and black individuals accounted for 0.5%.[9]

In the predominantly white community of Helena, Riley encountered the harsh realities of life with both darker skin and a disability. These circumstances posed significant hurdles for him and forced Ron and me to confront difficult truths. At the ages of five and three, Riley and Lexi were too young to comprehend his diagnosis and the complexities of their ethnicity fully. At that tender age, children tend to engage with others their own age, especially within the neighborhood.

We cherished our neighborhood, and I knew we had chosen the right community for our children to grow up in. After living in the neighborhood for a while, we became acquainted with most of the parents. As I was mostly home with my kids, it was essential for me to cultivate good relations with our neighbors. I felt more at ease when the neighbor kids came to our house to play. Initially, this arrangement worked well for us.

As Riley and Lexi began exploring the world around them, they desired more opportunities for play. They were permitted to visit a neighbor's house if I knew the parents and received their consent. Two young girls in the neighborhood occasionally came over to play. Since I had never met their parents, their house remained off-limits. Nevertheless, these girls seemed kind, and Riley and Lexi enjoyed their company.

One afternoon, Riley and Lexi rushed into the house in tears. They were crying profusely and struggled to articulate their words, their faces reflecting confusion and distress. Once I managed to calm them down, I asked what had upset them. They explained that they could no longer play with the two girls down the street. When I inquired why, they responded that it was because they were "Injun" and because Riley had *MS* (*multiple sclerosis*).

It was truly astonishing and hurtful when Riley was taunted and accused of having *multiple sclerosis* because he faced difficulties walking and playing like other kids. While some parents in the neighborhood were aware of his disability, we were not prepared to announce it to the world. However, it's important to note that Riley did not have *MS*; he had *Duchenne muscular dystrophy* (*DMD*). The misinformation surrounding his condition was deeply troubling to us, and we were determined to set the record straight.

This was uncharted territory for our family, and it brought back memories of my own parents advising me, "Let Riley live a normal life and treat him as an equal. Never allow his disability to cloud your judgment about who he can become." We were resolute in our decision not to let his disability overshadow our assessment of his potential.

The behavior of those parents was particularly upsetting because it included the use of racial slurs, such as the term "Injun," which is derogatory towards Native Americans and was directed at Riley and Lexi due to their darker skin. The ignorance displayed by these parents, who assumed the children must be Native American based on their skin color, was incomprehensible. Moreover, telling Riley and Lexi they were no longer welcome in their yard was utterly disgusting!

It is important to emphasize that everyone can have different diseases, and the color of one's skin does not determine their race. Blanket accusations and discrimination at such a young age can be incredibly detrimental and are based on pure naivety. It was difficult to understand why these neighbor parents acted so hostile and racist, refusing to allow their children to play with my children simply because Riley had physical limitations. It was even more perplexing how the color of anyone's skin played a role in this situation. To this day, it still makes my blood boil.

There's a common saying, "Don't punish the innocent. They know not what they say." I believed this to be true in this situation, as the children were merely parroting their parents' words. Wiping away those crocodile tears and reassuring them they did nothing wrong was heart-wrenching. Riley, being young, didn't fully understand what was happening to his body, and Lexi, at just three years old, could barely grasp why they couldn't play with these two girls anymore.

After much reflection and despite our anger, we decided not to kill the messenger but to respond with kindness. From then on, those children were only allowed to come over and play at our house and yard under our supervision. We never had any issues moving forward. It's worth mentioning that we never had the opportunity to meet or talk to these parents, even to this day.

Unfortunately, this would not be the last time Riley faced criticism and discrimination due to his disability. There are two other incidents that stand out in my memory. The first incident occurred during a chorus class, where Riley faced mistreatment from a classmate. In middle school, students had the choice to participate in either band or chorus. During the first year, Riley decided to join the band and play the clarinet. As a fellow clarinet player, I was thrilled because I played the same instrument in my younger days. I had chosen it because my older brother Dave had played it when he was in middle school.

Initially, Riley enjoyed playing the clarinet and practiced diligently. The music teacher started with simple songs and introduced more complex pieces requiring intricate finger movements. I could see Riley struggling to cover the holes with his fingers, and his face would turn red with each blow to the instrument. Riley's condition, *DMD*, affects all his muscles, including those surrounding his lungs. Inhaling and exhaling were always more laborious for him. Despite the complications, he persisted in playing until he became lightheaded. I realized that I needed to have a heart-to-heart conversation with him because it was evident he couldn't continue this way.

I was nervous when I had to talk to Riley about this because he never gave up easily. He had a stubborn streak, which I considered to be an admirable trait that had kept him going all these years. His motto was "Never give up! Never surrender!" But this time, he agreed that playing the clarinet was taking a toll on his body, and it was time to move on. Whenever he tried something new that didn't work out, he would say, "You can't say I didn't try. I gave it my best shot, but my best wasn't good enough this time. Let's try something new." And that was the end of his clarinet journey.

I called the school to explain the situation, and they were understanding and accommodating. They were able to transfer Riley to chorus instead. Just like that, Riley transitioned to chorus. This is where the story took an interesting turn. As Riley grew older, his disease progressed, but he could still walk without assistance and climb stairs if there was a railing for support. Unbeknownst to me, his chorus teacher assigned Riley to the second row on the chorus stage. However, Riley was much shorter than his peers due to his medications, which stunted his growth. Riley never informed his teacher about the difficulties he faced in reaching his spot because he needed a railing. His stubbornness got the better of him this time.

After two months of attending chorus, I received an email from his teacher expressing concern about Riley's absence from class for the past two weeks. This raised alarm bells in my mind. *What the hell is going on here*? I dropped him off at school every day and picked him up afterward. Riley was an excellent student who took pride in his academic achievements. Without hesitation, I logged into the school's parent portal and checked the absentee tab I had overlooked. To my surprise, Riley had attended every class except Chorus for the past two weeks. It suddenly clicked in my head. Riley had taken matters into his own hands and decided to deal with the problem on his own.

When Riley returned home from school that day, I asked him where he had been instead of attending chorus class. He replied that he had been going to the library to do his homework. Occasionally, Riley was allowed to visit the library when he couldn't participate in certain activities due to his *DMD*, and the librarian never questioned his motives.

Curious to know more, I probed further and asked why he had been skipping class. Riley revealed that a boy behind him had been harassing and poking him. Just because he was the smallest kid in school and had *DMD* didn't mean he would allow himself to be bullied. Riley had fought back but kept getting in trouble even though it wasn't his fault. Additionally, he had difficulty walking up the two steps to stand in his row. He chose not to attend class because it was too much of a hassle. "The Beast" was back, causing chaos and havoc.

I was determined that my son would not be bullied into skipping class. I refused to let his disability deprive him of a well-rounded education like his peers. Without delay, I called the teacher to inform him that Riley would be attending class every day from then on. We discussed the situation and devised a simple plan. The teacher moved Riley to the bottom row, and he kept a close eye on Riley's interactions with the bullying student. From then on, Riley was no longer bothered and could complete the chorus class.

In high school, the same student who had given Riley a hard time in chorus became his friend. People change and grow, and some learn from their past mistakes. That day marked a turning point in my relationship with Riley as well. He had overcome his hesitance to accept my assistance when he required it, and our communication regarding such situations became more open and effortless.

Regrettably, Riley would encounter several other hiccups that were squashed quickly. However, this last occurrence stands out as a significant problem as I tried to help Riley steer his ship through troubled waters. Riley had always been an excellent student and took great pride in his academic performance. When he entered high school, he was granted permission to use the elevator to attend classes on different floors. All of Riley's teachers were informed in advance about his early departure from class to use the elevator, ensuring he wouldn't be late for his next class.

One teacher had difficulty understanding and accepting this arrangement. Throughout the year, this teacher made Riley's life unnecessarily difficult. He constantly questioned Riley's work ethic, and they frequently clashed on various matters. One day, after a particularly exhausting conversation with this teacher, Riley prepared to leave the classroom to use the elevator. In front of everyone, the teacher publicly criticized him, saying, "I don't understand why you always need to use the elevator. You seem perfectly fine to me!" That was the straw that broke the camel's back!

Riley returned home feeling humiliated and embarrassed by the lack of empathy displayed by this teacher. I had personally reached my limit as well. I promptly contacted the teacher and confronted him about his behavior. I made it clear that he had no right to call out my son publicly. I then asked if he even knew why Riley had been granted permission to use the elevator. To my surprise, he had no knowledge of the reason. I proceeded to explain that a memo had been sent to all teachers at the beginning of the year, providing detailed information about Riley's condition and the reasons behind his elevator usage. I went into a lengthy explanation about Riley's *DMD* and the implications of his disability. I also mentioned that Riley had an *Individualized Education Program* (*IEP*), which required each teacher to familiarize themselves with his needs and those of other students in the class. The teacher was left speechless, as he had been called out and had no response. Fortunately, Riley managed to complete the rest of the school year without further repercussions.

Throughout Riley's high school years, he continued to face other challenges. However, due to his strong determination and willingness to stand up for himself in the face of adversity, he ultimately became the master of his own destiny.

We encountered numerous instances of prejudice and discrimination, even within the medical field. We confronted these problems head-on, fully aware that it would be an uphill battle.

Life Goes On

While settling into our new home in Helena, I closely monitored Riley's development in various aspects - socially, emotionally, and physically - and assured him that I would be there for him whenever he needed me. At the same time, I recognized the importance of spending quality time with Lexi, ensuring she felt comfortable and secure in her new environment.

To our delight, Riley adapted exceptionally well to the structured school environment at preschool. He quickly integrated with his peers and made himself at home. Ron and I felt immensely proud of his progress. Witnessing Riley's success and knowing that Lexi was also adjusting well in Helena gave me the confidence to begin searching for a part-time teaching job.

Fortunately, I secured a part-time teaching position at another preschool the following year when one of the teachers went on maternity leave. I even enrolled Riley in one of the classes at this new preschool, allowing him to be with me. While Riley thrived in this new school, he yearned for his friends from *Early Movement Preschool*.

As luck would have it, *Early Movement Preschool* became available for purchase the following year. Ron and I managed to scrape together the necessary funds and bought the preschool. This purchase fulfilled a lifelong dream for me - owning my own preschool, which proved valuable beyond words. It meant I could teach part-time while handling administrative work from home.

By the time I acquired *Early Movement Preschool*, Riley had already completed two years of preschool. Our local elementary school, *Rossiter Elementary School*, offered a Pre-K class, and I decided to enroll Riley in the morning session. In the afternoons, he would join me at the preschool. Lexi also accompanied me during this time, giving us the best of both worlds. I knew it would entail hard work, but Ron and I were willing to take on this exciting endeavor and move the business forward.

I felt the need to ensure that Riley's needs were met with minimal disruption during his school years. While he kept up socially with his peers, I knew he might require additional support mentally and physically due to his confirmed diagnosis of *DMD*.

I felt anxious about Riley's upcoming transition. It meant he would be entering a traditional school environment, surrounded by children from kindergarten to 5th grade. My goal was to provide a stable and long-term educational setting for both Riley and Lexi throughout their elementary school journey. Before the school year began, I met with Riley's teacher and the administration to discuss how we could assist Riley in transitioning to elementary school.

Recognizing Riley's unique learning style and challenges, I chose to enroll him in Pre-K instead of kindergarten. I believed an additional school year would boost his confidence and help him adjust to his condition. The wheels were set in motion, and Ron and I could only hope for the best while preparing for any obstacles that might arise.

Boys with *DMD* produce less than 3% dystrophin[10], a critical protein for muscle growth. Riley's minuscule amount of dystrophin posed a challenge as the brain is also a form of muscle. Despite this, he excelled as a student. However, his approach to learning and retaining information differed from that of most children. Riley often needed to repeat tasks in a rote manner until he grasped them, but once he did, he never forgot.

There were moments of frustration when he would say, "I know how to do this, but my brain gets stuck." Ron and I learned to be patient during these learning experiences. After several repetitions, we would witness the "aha" moment as Riley finally understood the concept. His sense of accomplishment was evident, knowing that once he learned something, it stayed with him.

As a preschool teacher, I noticed that Riley's learning and writing processes differed from his peers. While in Pre-K, I realized he would benefit from a tutor. Sometimes, a child responds better to another adult than to their own parent. Coincidentally, the teacher next door to my preschool taught at a Christian elementary school and was fantastic with young children. She and Riley formed an instant connection, and she became his tutor. One of Riley's struggles was holding a pencil correctly for writing. He would clench it with his fist instead of gripping it like we do. His tutor came up with a brilliant yet simple solution - she placed tiny dots on the pencil where his thumb and fingers should go. What a brilliant but simple and effective technique. This helped him learn how to hold the pencil correctly through repeated exercises until it became automatic. I informed his Pre-K teacher about this, and she was thoroughly impressed.

During that same year, Riley's Pre-K teacher requested a meeting with us. She expressed concern about Riley's work, particularly his reluctance to write his name on his papers. She believed he was not progressing as he should. I knew Riley could write his name, as I had witnessed him do it before. I decided to handle the situation myself.

I called Riley over to the table where we were discussing the matter. I asked him, "Riley, can you write your name?"

He confidently replied, "Yes, I can."

"Write your name on this paper," I replied.

He wrote his name without hesitation.

The teacher said, "You know, Riley, I have all these papers, and they don't have your name on them."

He looked at her and said, "That's because you didn't ask me to do it."

64

She told him, "Okay, so from now on, Riley, can you write your name on your paper?" He said, "Yes."

From then on, she made it a point to tell the class, "Write your name on your paper." He never had a problem again.

She was also perplexed about how to help him understand multiple directions. Whenever she gave the class more than one instruction at a time, he would just give her a blank stare. I explained to her that Riley could only process one direction at a time and would become overwhelmed if she went too fast. The frustration was evident on his face, so she agreed to slow down with her instructions.

I shared a "grounding" technique that Riley's tutor used with him. Whenever Riley started to get upset or fixated on something, she would approach him and place her hand on his shoulder. This would help him snap out of it and refocus on the task at hand. This method proved to be successful throughout Riley's time in grade school.

Seeing how well it worked, I began implementing the grounding technique at home with both Riley and Lexi. I even used it repeatedly at my preschool. Sometimes, simply having a calm presence and placing a hand on someone's shoulder can make all the difference.

That was just the beginning of our journey to understanding Riley's unique way of processing information and thinking. It's not uncommon for people to shy away from what they perceive as different. As a result, we always equip Riley with the necessary tools to handle various situations because we know we won't always be there to assist him.

Riley continued to thrive in Pre-K and Kindergarten with the techniques I shared with his teachers. However, I knew he would require even more support as he entered first grade. It was clear that Riley needed an *Individualized Education Program* (*IEP*). The *IEP* committee, which consisted of his teachers, the vice principal, the principal, the counselors, and us as parents, devised a plan.

I relied on this community of professionals to support Riley. As parents, we advocated for him and worked alongside his teachers. Having the *IEP* in place ensured that Riley would receive the necessary assistance to learn and grow in a school environment. I wanted his teachers to understand his unique needs and be mindful that his thinking processes differed from those of most students. Recognizing that teachers have many other students to attend to, I made it clear that I was always available to support them. Before each school year started, I would meet with his teachers to discuss his accommodations. This *IEP* would remain in effect until he graduated from high school. It required persistence and handling each situation with care. Always remember that those trying to help have the best intentions, but as parents, we know our children best.

Riley went on to have a tremendously successful academic career because we started early on to ensure that he could be the best version of himself. We never told him he couldn't do something or used the word "can't." To us, we were breaking new ground in how to support our child with *Duchenne*. We were pushing boundaries, and Riley was accomplishing things we were initially told he would never be capable of. For instance, we were told:

- **Riley would never be able to ride a bike**, but not only did he ride one, he did so without training wheels.
- **Riley should never participate in water sports**, but he learned how to kneeboard and went tubing behind our boat.
- **Riley should never jump on a trampoline**, but he defied that logic and continued jumping on a trampoline until high school.
- **Riley should never ski**, but he proved them wrong by skiing once, though he ultimately decided that his body couldn't handle it.

Children are often smarter and wiser than their years. Given the opportunity, their ability to do things can profoundly impact their lives and change how they perceive the world. It is important for them to have a say in how they want to live their lives. We discussed and adapted accordingly, allowing Riley to determine his own limits. By doing so, we could proceed with confidence, knowing what he was capable of.

Power of Positive Thinking – Raini's Story

"People come into your life for a reason, a season, or a lifetime."[11] Brian A. Chalker's words resonate deeply with the many experiences we encounter in life. People enter and exit our lives, but sometimes, even within a short period, they can shine their light the brightest when we need them the most. This rings true when I think of Ron's first cousin, Raini Aumueller.

Raini stepped into our lives during a time when we were grappling with how to manage Riley's diagnosis. We were uncertain about how to help Riley comprehend his illness and find solace. At the tender age of five, Riley had limited understanding of the challenges his body was facing.

Raini, the nephew of Ron's mother, Inge, was raised by his mother, Hilde, in Oregon. Inge and Hilde shared a close bond as the only two siblings. Ron had spent some formative years with Aunt Hilde's family. In the summer of 1997, Raini visited our family in Montana, and we decided to take him boating on Canyon Ferry Lake.

During the boat ride, Riley became captivated by the necklace adorning Raini's neck. It was a crystal pendant encased by a snake, elegantly coiled around the crystal, and resting against Raini's chest. Riley was fascinated by how it seemed to fit perfectly.

It was during this boat ride that Ron disclosed Riley's diagnosis to Raini. Ron sensed that Raini had faced his own share of hardships, and he felt compelled to share Riley's story. The news deeply affected Raini.

After the boat ride, Raini knelt, unclasped the snake necklace from his own neck, and placed it around Riley's. He explained to Riley how significant the necklace was to him and believed that Riley would take good care of it. Raini knew it would serve as a source of strength for Riley whenever he needed it most.

In Raini's own words, he eloquently expressed the profound meaning behind this act of selflessness and his decision to share something he held dear with someone he believed needed it more than he did.

Raini's Story

"I have been fascinated by gemstones and crystals, so it was no surprise when I stopped at a local flea market. A cart was sparkling with many crystals, including sapphires and amethyst. A certain necklace caught my eye, as it had a sky-blue crystal wrapped with a silver cobra snake. Since I was also into collecting and restoring classic Shelby Ford Mustangs and A/C Cobras, I was instantly drawn to it."

"Over several years, I had many serious accidents and medical issues. I was pronounced dead twice and managed to come back. All the while, I wore the necklace. When nervous, I held the crystal in my hand and drug it back and forth on the silver chain. After wearing out many chains, I changed it to a simple piece of black woven cordage."

"On my 30th birthday in 1987, my girlfriend surprised me by taking me to Disneyland for a week. Although I was grateful, I didn't feel well. Upon coming home and returning to work, I was very agitated by my best friend, who was like a mosquito; you can't swat. He followed me around bitching about everything until I grabbed him around his throat with my left hand, lifted him a foot off the ground, and was ready to punch him with my right. I was suddenly shocked to realize what I had almost done. As I apologized, my friend said I looked through him as if he wasn't even there."

"I immediately contacted my doctor, who would not tell me the results of my blood tests and only referred me to a specialist who told me that I had a large cancerous tumor in my chest. I told my girlfriend and her family, who immediately moved me into her house since it was closer to the hospital. The oncologist warned me that the chemotherapy was extreme, and it might even kill me before the cancer did. I told him I had too many people counting on me, things I still want to do, and places to see."

"I spent nearly three years in and out of the hospital treatment center and x-ray department. The snake and crystal helped keep my mind off what was happening to me the whole time. At one point, I was going downhill fast and had to go in for surgery. I wouldn't let the doctor remove my necklace, and the nurse wrapped it in gauze and taped it to my neck. I woke up halfway through the surgery and was trying to hold my necklace; they strapped my arms to the table and sedated me even more."

"After the surgery, the doctor came in and informed me that they had great difficulty and I had been pronounced dead, but my heart started beating again, and they were able to finish. He said there was no medical reason that he could find explaining that I was still alive."

"The nurse removed the trach tube and the gauze from my snake. She was amazed that the crystal was no longer sapphire blue but had turned solid black. It would later turn to blue again."

"I have no idea either, but after word got around, the chaplain came to see me and asked me if I would be willing to talk to his congregation about my ordeal and experience in the afterlife. I explained that I experienced a bright white light, but it was just someone prying my eyelids open and shining a flashlight into my eyes. And when I felt a force holding me back, I assumed it was the doctor since I hadn't paid my bill yet. Don't get me wrong, I have no idea if crystals or a piece of colored glass have any powers, but the power of positive thought is probably 90% of the cure."

"I gave the necklace to Riley while I was visiting Montana. My intention was not to give false hope but rather a way to redirect attention away from the ailment and onto more positive thoughts."

The necklace held great significance for Riley, who had been wearing it since age five. Even at such a tender age, receiving the necklace meant the world to him. He would describe the object as a magical crystal possessing extraordinary healing abilities. Riley strongly believes in the power of positive thinking, and this belief has been instrumental in his perseverance over the years. Throughout his life, this necklace has provided him with solace during difficult times. Similar to Raini, who clung to the necklace as a source of strength during dark days, Riley never removes it from around his neck. We have gone through several chains and even conducted minor repairs on the snake pendant to ensure the crystal remains intact. Its sentimental value and associated memories made it a cherished possession throughout his life.

The act of Raini giving Riley that necklace was truly transformative for us. It became a significant event in our lives, as it instilled in Riley a newfound confidence, willpower, and a positive outlook on life. At that moment, he realized he could surpass the limitations imposed by his condition. It made him believe that he could accomplish more than just a young boy grappling with this disease. I firmly believe that this gift played a substantial role in his perseverance over the years.

Riley's positivity and perspective on life are truly remarkable. The world would undoubtedly be better if everyone could possess even a fraction of his optimism.

Ron and I have consistently emphasized the power of positivity. We firmly believe in maintaining a positive mindset and striving to normalize things as much as possible. This philosophy has become our guiding principle, shaping the way we approach life's challenges.

Lexi

What can I say about Lexi? I cannot find the right words to express how much she means to us. Lexi continues to be a guiding light in our lives, like a beacon of hope shining through a distant tunnel. Her presence fills us with immense pride and joy.

People often remark about Riley, saying, "He's doing so well. You guys are doing an amazing job." And yes, we are doing our best, but there is so much more to it. Sometimes, in a family, other children can unintentionally be left behind. It's not the fault of the parents. *DMD* is an all-consuming disease that demands a significant amount of time and attention from parents. It becomes necessary to prioritize our entire lives around it.

I had the unique experience of growing up in a household where two out of my three brothers had *spinal muscular dystrophy* (*SMA*). I was able to apply that knowledge and carry it forward when I had Riley. That's why, when we were blessed with the arrival of Lexi, I knew we would never leave her behind.

Lexi was born, a tiny bundle of pure sunshine, weighing a little over six pounds when we brought her home. She was so small that she had to

70

wear preemie clothes. I wanted Lexi to possess my mother's strength and fortitude. I wanted her to grow up to be resilient yet kind and compassionate. I wanted her to think for herself, question the world around her, and be a fighter who stands up for herself and never be afraid to speak her mind, just like my mom. It was crucial for us to ensure she never felt unloved and that she had the same opportunities to succeed.

Every day, I thank God for the timing of Lexi's arrival. I became pregnant with her when Riley was only 17 months old. It was truly a miracle because shortly after, we started noticing problems with Riley's health. Lexi might never have happened if we had waited a few more months to conceive. Fear would have held us back. We would have missed out on the incredible experience of bringing Lexi into this world. I know I wouldn't have had another child due to the fear of another unknown disease lurking in the background. So, fate played a significant role in that decision. You can call it divine intervention or anything you like, but for us, it was a gift from God.

As a young mother, I always dreamed of having two boys and one girl. When Lexi turned three, Ron and I knew we didn't want to take any more chances. Ron offered to have a vasectomy, but after his doctor canceled several appointments, we became frustrated. I made the decision to have a tubal ligation, as I knew I wouldn't have more children at the age of 29. It was an easy choice for me. After welcoming Lexi into our lives, we realized how truly blessed we were to have her. She seamlessly integrated into our family and became an irreplaceable part of our lives. I scheduled the procedure, and two weeks later, it was done. I have never regretted that decision. With that enormous weight lifted off my shoulders, I could focus on what mattered most: taking care of the best kids a mother could ask for.

From the moment she was born, Riley loved her unconditionally. He was always attentive and cherished every minute of growing up with her. With only 26 months between them, they were close enough in age to be playmates and develop a deep sibling bond.

Even at a young age, Lexi was amazing. Although she may not have fully understood or been able to articulate it, she knew that Riley was different and that she needed to be there for him. Lexi always looked up to him and wanted to emulate everything he did. She even potty trained herself at 23 months, inspired by her big brother. She quickly followed suit whenever she saw Riley accomplish something, like tying his shoes or getting dressed. She was curious, thoughtful, and always eager to help.

Ron had a nightly exercise routine with Riley as part of his physical therapy. Riley's calves and ankles would tighten, and Ron would stretch him out. Lexi would lie right beside them, and after Ron finished with Riley, Lexi would eagerly say, "Now it's my turn, Daddy. Do my exercises like Riley." Ron would then stretch Lexi out, just like her big brother. It became a special bonding experience for all of them. We included her in any way we could and never excluded her.

Riley and Lexi, being close in age, found comfort in each other's presence. We encouraged them to rely on one another, and it became apparent when Riley was around six years old that he would seek solace in Lexi's room during the night whenever he felt unwell or had a bad dream. Lexi would willingly welcome him, and we would often discover them peacefully snuggled together in the morning. Although we were aware of this ritual, we chose not to intervene, as it seemed they were fostering a sense of self-reliance. This bond would prove invaluable for Riley as he faced the challenges of living with *DMD*.

The love between Lexi and her brother was evident, and Riley adored her. Riley would selflessly defer to Lexi whenever decisions needed to be made, allowing her to take the spotlight. It was his way of diverting attention from himself and ensuring her happiness.

At times, Riley had ulterior motives for encouraging Lexi to try new things. When he felt uncertain due to the limitations imposed by his condition, he would nudge Lexi to attempt them first. Despite not always understanding his intentions, Lexi always embraced these challenges with a positive attitude. If Lexi succeeded, Riley would find the courage to follow suit. She was his ever-reliable partner in crime, and I always admired the strength of their bond. Riley knew he could count on Lexi, just as she knew he would always strive to protect her.

We made a conscious effort to balance our attention and prioritize Lexi's needs to ensure she never felt overshadowed. We acknowledged that Riley's needs often required more immediate attention, not because of any fault of his own but due to the nature of his disease. Lexi grasped this concept remarkably well, displaying wisdom beyond her years.

Nevertheless, it was sometimes challenging for her, as she could only comprehend so much. Living in someone else's shadow can present difficulties, yet Lexi handled it with grace and poise. She has grown into a remarkable woman, embodying integrity, passion, kindness, and understanding.

Mom Guilt

I have been going through a period of deep introspection and reflection. I have found myself questioning my impact on others and the pain I may have caused. As someone who strongly identifies with my Catholic upbringing, I have been grappling with feelings of extreme guilt and a sense of responsibility for the suffering of those around me. It can be incredibly challenging to open up to others, unsure of how they will react to the truths we hold within ourselves. I have often believed that I can handle everything on my own without needing the assistance or support of others.

However, upon reflection, I realize that this mindset was merely a facade. It is essential to recognize that it is perfectly acceptable and even necessary to ask for help, even if the response we receive may not align with our expectations. The title of John Gray's book, *Men Are from Mars, Women Are from Venus*[12], rings true in many ways. Women possess a maternal instinct that drives us to care for and protect those we love dearly, often to the point of sacrificing our own mental and physical well-being. The need to shield our loved ones is a constant presence in the lives of mothers.

Ron's mother, Inge, had a deep love for both Riley and Lexi. She cherished the opportunity to care for them twice a week and relished every chance she had to spend time with them. Being a grandmother was a role she took seriously, and she enjoyed showering them with affection. Riley held a special place in her heart as her first grandson, and she loved him wholeheartedly.

Inge had a keen sense that Ron and I were going through a rough patch. She could tell that something was amiss with Riley but never pushed us to tell her. We found ourselves continuously postponing the difficult task of informing her about Riley's diagnosis.

We knew we were going to have to tell her but were hesitant to share this life-altering news with her, fearing the devastation it might cause. Having witnessed my mother's reaction to similar news, we knew it would be an arduous conversation to have. As the situation unfolded, I felt a strong sense of obligation to inform Inge about Riley's condition, especially considering her role as the caregiver for the children. It was important for us to share this information with her now that we had received a definitive diagnosis.

I vividly remember the day we visited Inge's house to pick up the kids. We knew it was time to have this serious conversation. Ron took the lead and began explaining that the test results had indeed confirmed Riley's diagnosis of *Duchenne muscular dystrophy*. He detailed what this meant for Riley's future and the treatment plans we had in place. As expected, Inge struggled with the news and reassured us that everything would be okay.

We left feeling a profound sense of emptiness, knowing we had shattered her heart. Delivering such news is always heart-wrenching.

Several hours later, we received a life-altering phone call. Ron's sister informed us that Inge had been rushed to the hospital. She was having difficulty speaking, and her words seemed nonsensical. An ambulance transported her to the hospital, where it was discovered that she had suffered a mini-stroke.

At that moment, I was overwhelmed with guilt and began to cry, believing that I had caused her stroke. It was my idea to have the conversation with Inge, and we had struggled to find the right time for it. The weight of guilt consumed me, and I was convinced that the news had been too much for her to bear. As a Catholic, I was well-acquainted with carrying guilt, and I blamed myself for this tragedy.

Inge's doctors conducted several tests and concluded she had likely experienced mini-strokes for some time. She was ultimately diagnosed with *glioblastoma multiforme*, an aggressive and fast-growing brain tumor.

During this time, Inge was too ill to inquire much about Riley's condition. Likewise, Riley, being so young, didn't ask many questions about his grandmother's cancer. Their love for each other remained unconditional, and that's what truly mattered.

Ron and his siblings provided excellent care for her until she passed away a year later. In 1999, when Riley was just 7 years old, we lost her. We felt fortunate that Riley and Lexi had the time they did with their grandmother, who was loving, caring, and an exceptional mother to all.

I often find myself thinking about Inge, and the guilt lingers like an open wound rubbed with salt. I wish I hadn't pushed Ron to tell her about Riley's diagnosis. She didn't live that long after that, and maybe I could have spared her that pain.

As a mother, my primary role was to protect her, and I feel remorse for inflicting such hurt upon her. I despise "The BEAST" for that.

Parent Project Muscular Dystrophy

After Riley was diagnosed with *DMD*, Ron took it upon himself to conduct extensive research on the disease. Due to my brothers' conditions, we were already familiar with the *Muscular Dystrophy Association* (*MDA*), which covers a wide range of *Muscular dystrophies*. However, Ron understood the importance of finding a group or association specifically dedicated to *DMD* to ensure Riley received the best possible medical care.

After countless searches and many sleepless nights, Ron came across the *Parent Project Muscular Dystrophy* (*PPMD*). It was exactly the organization we had been looking for. Ron reached out to Pat Furlong, and we attended our first *PPMD* Conference at UCLA in Los Angeles.

"*Parent Project Muscular Dystrophy* was founded in 1994 by President and CEO Pat Furlong and a group of parents and grandparents who were frustrated by the lack of investment in *Duchenne* research. When doctors diagnosed her two sons, Christopher and Patrick, with *Duchenne* in 1984, Pat didn't accept "there's no hope and little help" as an answer. *Duchenne* is the most common fatal genetic childhood disorder, which affects approximately 1 out of every 3,500 boys each year worldwide. It currently has no cure."

"With Pat at the helm, *Parent Project Muscular Dystrophy* began, working to understand the pathology of the disorder, the extent of research investment, and the mechanisms for optimal care. Her sons lost their battle with *Duchenne* in their teenage years, but her fight continues on behalf of all families affected by *Duchenne muscular dystrophy*."[13]

Parent Project Muscular Dystrophy is a grassroots organization recognized around the world. There is now better access to care and approved therapies, and research continues to move forward with new legislation to fund research and outreach programs.[14]

At this juncture in our lives, we were essentially flying blindly through Riley's condition. We were both nervous and excited about attending the conference, as we knew there was so much we could learn. Living in Montana provided limited opportunities for the specialized care required for *DMD*. We approached the conference with open minds and a strong eagerness to connect with doctors, therapists, scientists, and other parents who could provide valuable insights.

Boy, did we learn a lot! There was so much information to take in; it was overwhelming! From the first day, we knew this was exactly where we needed to be. The professionals we encountered were at the top of their game and well-versed in the latest advancements in *Duchenne muscular dystrophy*.

We returned from the conference feeling invigorated and excited to implement some of the knowledge we had gained. The discussions at the conference emphasized not only treating the body with medication but also focusing on the mind, body, and soul. Consequently, we decided to explore alternative therapies for Riley. We took him for acupuncture, sought the help of a massage therapist, and consulted a naturopath who conducted muscle tests. The naturopath recommended bee pollen, which Riley consumed for several months. Additionally, Ron had a friend who treated water with a reverse osmosis machine, and based on Riley's height and weight, he drank the prescribed amount of this dense water daily.

Some people may have thought we were crazy, but we saw it as being proactive. *Duchenne muscular dystrophy* was "The Beast" that Riley faced daily, and we were willing to try anything to improve his quality of life. We were cautious about not compromising his health in other ways and kept an open mind about treatment options. Riley knew that his parents would go to any lengths to help him, and we embraced a fearless attitude. We tried every possible avenue, taking his young age into consideration. This mindset played a crucial role in his resilience as he grew older, and we were committed to giving him every advantage he deserved.

We understood the importance of keeping Riley active while preserving his limited muscle function. We frequently visited Ron's family cabin at Canyon Ferry Lake in Helena, MT, and even purchased a boat so Riley and Lexi could engage in physical activities together.

Developing Riley's lung function and respiratory system was particularly important. He participated in group swimming lessons to keep his muscles engaged and later transitioned to private lessons for more individual attention. As a young child, he also underwent hydrotherapy. By being proactive from the start, these activities greatly benefited him and addressed potential future concerns.

As *PPMD* was still in its infancy, it required funding for research. Ron felt compelled to dive headfirst into supporting *PPMD* in any way possible. One of their fundraising programs involved distributing canisters with the *PPMD* logo. Ron believed this was an effective way for us to contribute. We received 50 canisters and placed them in various businesses around Helena, Montana. We took turns visiting each store every other week to check if the cans needed to be emptied. We collected the money and sent a check to *PPMD*. This canister program was a success and helped raise awareness about *Duchenne muscular dystrophy* within the community. As time went on, *PPMD* transitioned to other fundraising efforts, and we were proud of our contributions. We had a good run!

When Riley turned seven, Ron and I attended another *PPMD* conference, where doctors and colleagues emphasized the importance of being proactive in Riley's care. They suggested putting him on steroids to help maintain his limited muscle function. During a roundtable discussion, the use of steroids in treating boys with *DMD* was brought up. Although we had been primarily exploring Eastern medicine options, we became curious about what Western medicine had to offer for Riley's condition. The doctors mentioned prednisone, a widely used steroid in the U.S., but we were hesitant due to its numerous harmful side effects such as weight gain, moon face, anger, excessive eating, and psychological concerns.

In our search for an alternative to prednisone, we came across a doctor in Canada who was treating *DMD* patients with a corticosteroid called *Deflazacort*. He spoke about its fewer side effects compared to prednisone and the positive reactions seen in boys. Deflazacort seemed like a promising option for Riley. The only snafu was that it wasn't *FDA*-approved in the U.S. It had been used for decades in Canada, and the results were very encouraging. We placed our trust in our *PPMD* community and the associated doctors, which gave us a sense of reassurance and confidence in our decision-making process. It is crucial to have faith in the medical professionals who are part of our healthcare journey, as they play a vital role in providing us with the necessary care and guidance. The doctor's expertise and the positive feedback from other parents, professionals, and other doctors convinced us to give steroids a try.

The Canadian doctor we met possessed an upbeat and humorous personality. He consistently urged parents not to take things too seriously. Despite the challenging circumstances of dealing with a life-threatening disease, he consistently encouraged us to make time for enjoyment. He emphasized the importance of being present with our children and finding opportunities for fun.

I remember one incident after his talk when a parent in the audience asked about giving their child Vitamin D supplements. The doctor humorously replied, "If you're Vitamin D deficient, you need to go outside in the sun and eat some chocolate." The room erupted in laughter, and it helped alleviate some of the tension. It highlighted the need for humor in the medical field.

Ron and I made a conscious effort not to take everything too seriously and to enjoy our time with Riley. Even now, 24 years later, we still laugh about that moment.

Our primary goal was to preserve Riley's mobility for as long as possible. With the support of the doctor in Canada and our care team at *PPMD*, we started Riley on *Deflazacort* when he was seven and a half years old. We had to have it shipped to us monthly from Canada. While many parents we met at the conference used *Deflazacort* or *Prednisone* on weekends, every other day, or once a week, we were advised that using it daily with Riley would yield the best results. Our intuition told us to commit to this treatment fully; it was all or nothing, so we chose to administer it daily. *Deflazacort* helped sustain Riley's mobility and gave him the strength to walk unassisted until he was 22.

During the *PPMD* conference, doctors recommended that Riley undergo a *DEXA* Scan to assess his bone density and determine his bone age. We were surprised that this was necessary at such a young age, but *PPMD* emphasized the importance of being proactive. Boys with *Duchenne* are at risk of developing brittle bones and osteoporosis.

After returning home to Helena, we scheduled Riley's scan. When they called with the results, they informed me that he had severe osteoporosis. They cautioned us to be extremely careful as he could easily experience compression fractures and back or neck pain. They mentioned a Z score of -4.0, which was devastating news. I couldn't comprehend what was happening, but I knew someone who could help. I reached out to our friends in the medical field and shared our fears and concerns. They assured us they would investigate the matter on our behalf.

We didn't usually involve our friends in these issues, but this was important. We just needed some advice on how to proceed. They were more knowledgeable than us, and we trusted their opinion immensely.

True to their word, our friends promptly got back to us. It turned out that the chart had been misread. The radiologist had interpreted the results as if Riley were a 70-year-old woman, disregarding his age and gender when delivering the news. Our friends reassured us, saying, "We're going to help you." They connected us with a specialist in Seattle who dealt with pediatric osteoporosis, and he provided much-needed clarification. Considering Riley's age and the stage of his disease progression, the specialist explained that the situation was not as dire as we initially thought. He prescribed *Alendronate* (*Fosamax*) to address Riley's *osteoporosis*.

From that point on, we realized the importance of being cautious about who treated Riley and always seeking clarification when needed. We became experts on *DMD* because we intimately understood what Riley was going through. It was not uncommon to discover that, at times, we possessed more information on certain topics concerning Riley than some medical professionals.

We had complete confidence in the individuals associated with *PPMD,* as they had become integral to our lives. They provided us with the upmost support and were like a second family. Their presence and assistance were vital to our well-being and served as a crucial support network.

The Life of Riley

The photograph on the book cover captures a moment from Riley's childhood when he was nine years old, during a trip to Glacier Park, Montana. This is how I envisioned Riley living and feeling each day of his life. He was accompanied by my three brothers, Greg, Dave, and Chris, as well as Ron and my nephew Robert. My brother Chris came in from Las Vegas so they could all go together on this road trip. The trip was a special bonding experience for the guys. Riley cherished these moments spent with his male relatives, as they allowed him to feel a sense of normalcy and joy.

Ron, capturing the essence of Riley's happiness, took a picture of him with a wide smile and open arms, embracing the beautiful countryside without a worry in the world. It's a snapshot of pure bliss, evoking the carefree spirit every child should have at that age. At that moment, there is no *DMD*, no thoughts of doctor visits or medication, and no somber reflections on how to survive through the day. Ron and my brothers wished for Riley to experience this feeling of unbridled happiness every day, free from the burdens of his condition. They were willing to do anything to make him feel normal, even if only for a fleeting moment. The trip left them with a renewed perspective on life, allowing them to relive their own childhoods alongside Riley.

In the photograph, Riley is shirtless, as both he and my brother Chris decided that "real men" don't wear shirts during the trip (hahaha). I was later informed that the two of them went shirtless throughout the entire journey. When Riley grew tired, Chris would carry him around everywhere. It was a precious bonding experience for all of them. In our family, where life tends to be challenging, these memories become etched in our hearts forever. These special moments can last a lifetime.

As Riley continued to grow, Ron and my brothers took him on other trips. They traveled to Denver and Seattle, where Riley had the opportunity to watch his beloved football team, the Miami Dolphins, in action. They also attended baseball games and visited museums in the big cities. During these trips, if Riley felt tired, he would stand on the back of Uncle Buddy's (my brother Dave's) wheelchair. From a young age, Riley understood that a wheelchair was simply an extension of one's body. He understood that being in a wheelchair didn't signify the end of possibilities but that there was still plenty of fun. Another memorable adventure took them to Yellowstone Park, immersing themselves in the wonders of the great outdoors. These trips are still fondly remembered, and they often find themselves reminiscing about the good old days.

Sports have always played a significant role in Riley's life. From a young age, he was obsessed with sports and would spend countless hours watching games on television. Riley's passion for sports became a strong bond between him and Ron, especially during their out-of-town medical appointments.

Since I was busy caring for Lexi at home and running a preschool business, Ron was responsible for accompanying Riley to his medical appointments. Prior to each appointment, Ron would research available sporting events and secure tickets. He wanted Riley to have something to look forward to beyond routine medical visits. Additionally, Ron made it a point to take Riley to the finest restaurants they could find, turning these outings into memorable experiences.

Riley would take our bad days in a heartbeat because they could be his best days because we didn't have his disability. Our difficult day didn't appear so bleak when we viewed it from that perspective. It helped us realize that our own challenges weren't as insurmountable as they seemed. It was crucial for us to cultivate compassion and understanding and, most importantly, to practice patience.

A Home for Riley

When Riley was nine years old, we noticed that he was having difficulty walking up and down the stairs in our house. He would carefully take one step at a time from the kitchen to the downstairs family room. It became clear that it was time to consider a home without stairs. We began searching for pre-existing homes but soon realized that remodeling them to make them accessible would be just as costly as building a new home. We made the decision to look for land in the same school district since Riley had already established a strong network of friends, and I had developed a good relationship with his teachers. Riley had an *Individualized Education Program* (*IEP*) and was doing well academically, so we didn't want to disrupt his social and academic life.

Putting Riley's needs first has always been our priority, so building a handicap-accessible home seemed the most logical choice. Fortunately, we were able to find land to purchase in the same school district, which was a relief because we didn't want Riley to experience unnecessary changes. The routine was incredibly important for him, so we wanted to make the transition as smooth as possible. One minor inconvenience we encountered was that we listed our home for sale, and surprisingly, it sold faster than we anticipated. As a result, we had to temporarily move into a duplex until our new home was constructed. At that point in our lives, we were in a good place where we could finally take a breath and enjoy life a little.

Some people say that building a house can make or break a marriage. They believe that if a couple can successfully build a house without getting a divorce, then they can get through anything. Most people build their dream house focusing on aesthetics rather than practicality. The stress of going through construction, making decisions on house plans and so on, can be very taxing and draining. Ron and I had already been through so much with Riley that building a house turned out to be easier than expected. We had always prioritized our responsibilities towards Riley, and building this house was no different. We compartmentalized our roles and made sure that every aspect of the house would be Riley-friendly. We had to constantly consider the future and try to anticipate how his condition might progress with *Duchenne muscular dystrophy*. Our goal was to give Riley every opportunity to continue walking.

Luckily, my brothers lived nearby, and they were able to assist with the construction. We jokingly referred to them as our "guinea pigs" because we would test everything out on them during the building process. If they couldn't traverse certain areas in their wheelchairs, we would modify the construction plans accordingly. Their input was crucial, especially since Riley was still able to walk at that time.

With their help, we were able to figure out the optimal floor plan and ensure that everything flowed smoothly for Riley so that when he eventually transitioned to using a wheelchair, the house would be ready. We were fortunate to find a contractor who had experience building accessible living spaces for an organization called *West Mont*, which supports individuals with disabilities. Moving day came the day after Christmas in 2001, and up until that point, it had been one of the best decisions we had ever made.

Growing up and raising a child with a terminal disease like *DMD* can consume a significant amount of time and energy, both emotionally and physically. It requires you to let go of the dreams and expectations you had for a "normal" child and shift your focus towards new hopes and dreams for your child with special needs. We have come to understand that life with this disease is not hopeless; it's about learning to live with it. It's about teaching your child to accept themselves and their surroundings, nurturing them, and helping them grow. It's about instilling in them the belief that they can accomplish anything with the resources they have.

Duchenne muscular dystrophy doesn't become easier over time; it simply becomes different. As Riley has progressed through different stages of the disease, we have adapted alongside him. We are living this journey through him, doing everything in our power to lighten his burden and improve his quality of life.

There is HOPE! There is always HOPE!

Chapter 5: Riley's Heart

Riley Will Soon Need a New Heart

Making Memories

Riley faces daily challenges in performing basic tasks such as moving, getting out of bed, brushing his teeth, applying deodorant, and getting dressed. Despite his struggles, he strives to maintain his independence and prefers to do things on his own. While it would be quicker and easier for me to assist him, I respect his wishes and only intervene when necessary. Patience has become a key virtue in our daily lives, and both Ron and I deeply admire and support Riley's determination at age 14.

Given the terminal nature of *DMD*, we understood the importance of creating lasting memories while Riley still had mobility. We embarked on various excursions across the United States and abroad, exposing him and Lexi to different cultures, sporting events, and exotic locations within our means.

We took flights to various destinations, including Hawaii for snorkeling and deep-sea fishing, Disneyland, Disney World, Atlantis in the Bahamas, and Mexico to explore the ancient ruins in Tulum. We also took road trips to Glacier National Park for white-water rafting and Yellowstone National Park for horseback riding. We even drove down to Salt Lake City for the Winter Olympics.

Our trip to Lima, Peru, was one of his favorites. The kids wanted to visit the place where Ron's father grew up. We wanted Riley and Lexi to immerse themselves in history, savor local cuisine, and observe this beautiful country and its culture. Coming from the United States, we often overlook many privileges we enjoy. While in Peru, we ventured to Paracas, where we lodged at a resort with Ron's relatives. We embarked on a dune buggy tour to witness the vast dunes and even tried our hand at desert surfing. Ron and Riley arranged a flight over the Nazca Lines, a sight only visible from the sky. We visited the ancient mountaintop city of Machu Picchu and delved into the history of the Inca Empire. Riley was

Ron, Riley, Nina, Lexi

captivated by phenomena that seemed otherworldly. The city was built with thousands of steps. When Riley got too tired, Ron would carry him up and down the mountain.

We felt incredibly fortunate to offer these unforgettable journeys to our children. *DMD* was our rationale for indulging in these experiences.

Our travels weren't just about sightseeing; they were about immersing ourselves in new environments, savoring local cuisines, and understanding different ways of life. Each journey was a unique opportunity for our children to learn and grow, and we considered these adventures as investments in their personal development.

Hunting is a popular sport in Montana. Ron often went hunting with his dad and brothers, which was always a special bonding experience for them. Hunting with his dad was something Riley particularly enjoyed. Getting him out into the great outdoors was always a positive experience. Ron enrolled him in Hunter's safety classes, and the instructor knew of Riley's disability. Riley participated in all activities with the class, including field exercises and tests. Ron was there to provide support, and I'll be damned if he didn't do everything on his own and pass.

On November 29, 2003, at just eleven years old, Riley achieved a remarkable feat by shooting a buffalo. This was a fantastic achievement for any hunter. It was a moment of pure joy and amazement for Ron and Riley. Here is an eleven-year-old boy with *DMD* who is moving around independently without needing medical equipment, and he can still pursue his dreams. Ron had the meat processed and even had a buffalo rug made, which now adorns Riley's room. At age thirteen, he shot a huge mule deer buck, which his uncles affectionately called "Big Buck." It was mounted and hung in his room. Ron was keenly aware that there might come a time when Riley wouldn't be able to travel as much, and eventually, their hunting adventures might come to an end.

As Riley continues his journey with resilience and courage, we remain grateful for the precious moments we've shared and the lessons learned along the way. While we understand that circumstances may change in the future, we hold onto these memories as treasures that will forever shape Riley's outlook on life and his view of just how big and beautiful the world is.

Cardiomyopathy

Cardiomyopathy is a heart muscle disease that makes it more difficult for the heart to pump blood to the rest of the body and often leads to heart failure.

In the evenings, after putting the kids to bed, Ron would diligently research the latest developments in the field of *DMD*. He scoured the internet for information on clinical trials that Riley could potentially join, as well as any new treatment options that could slow down the progression of the disease. Our conversations often revolved around strategizing our next steps in combatting *DMD*. We were constantly seeking any possible way to provide a boost for Riley, no matter how small. Unfortunately, more often than not, our efforts did not yield tangible results.

Since Riley's diagnosis, there hasn't been a day when I haven't thought about it. I often question if I can do more to improve the situation or if I've already done enough. *DMD* has a way of consuming you, leaving you breathless at times. Sadly, for Riley, struggling for breath would soon become a harsh reality.

When Riley was ten, we attended another *Parent Project (PPMD) Conference*, where we met up with Pat Furlong and Dr. Linda Cripe. They both played a significant role in Riley's care and suggested it would be a good time to test for Cardiomyopathy to establish a baseline for Riley's heart health. Dr. Linda Cripe mentioned that this was a new practice they were implementing: regular heart checkups for boys with *DMD*. It was recommended we schedule these checkups annually from now on.

At age 10, Riley was thriving, and we were grateful for his well-being. However, now we had to confront the possibility of heart issues. It's frustrating how "The Beast" keeps throwing down the gauntlet. We inquired with Linda about the potential scenario of Riley needing a heart transplant.

Dr. Cripe explained, "Heart transplants for children with *DMD* are uncommon, and if Riley required one, the chances of survival would be slim due to the strenuous nature of the surgery. These tests could help identify suitable medications to manage any heart conditions he might have. Around 35% of *DMD* patients may develop Cardiomyopathy."

Attending this conference was truly an eye-opening experience. The process of having Riley checked for Cardiomyopathy caused us a great deal of stress. Various unsettling thoughts crossed our minds. What if he is diagnosed with Cardiomyopathy? How would we go about treating it? Who would be responsible for conducting the necessary tests? Perhaps we are already behind in providing him with the necessary care. Are we destined to face more problems and losses? The mere idea and significance of uncovering another symptom of this debilitating disease was truly staggering. We took solace in knowing we were in capable hands with Pat Furlong, Dr. Cripe, and the entire team of specialists at *Cincinnati Children's Hospital*.

We planned to conduct the testing in Montana and review the results with Riley's care team at *Cincinnati Children's Hospital (CCH)*. A traveling cardiologist from Great Falls, Montana, examined Riley and diagnosed him with mild Cardiomyopathy. Just as we were catching our breath, another issue arose. The recommendation was to start him on Digoxin. Upon researching this medication, we learned that it is commonly used to enhance the strength and efficiency of the heart or to regulate the heart's rate and rhythm. This can lead to improved blood circulation and reduced swelling in the hands and ankles for patients with heart conditions. We felt uncertain about initiating Digoxin for Riley without first consulting our care team.

Here we go again, the roller coaster that is our life. With Riley being diagnosed with Cardiomyopathy, this was a new concern we had to factor in. We reached out to Dr. Linda Cripe for guidance, and she told us, "No Digoxin for him; he needs to be on ace inhibitors and beta-blockers." Beta-blockers block specific chemicals from binding to nerve receptors in the heart, slowing the heart rate and reducing blood pressure. Additionally, blood thinners or anticoagulants are crucial for preventing the formation of blood clots, especially in children with the dilated form of Cardiomyopathy.

Angiotensin-converting enzyme inhibitors, also known as ACE inhibitors, are typically prescribed for individuals with heart failure characterized by reduced ejection fraction, such as dilated Cardiomyopathy. These medications work to widen or dilate blood vessels, enhancing blood flow. Dr. Cripe emphasized the importance of being proactive when it comes to managing Riley's condition due to *DMD*.

She recommended reaching out to Dr. James Wiggins, a highly respected pediatric cardiologist currently practicing in Billings, Montana. Having previously worked under him, she spoke highly of his expertise and care.

With the assistance of the *Parent Project for Muscular Dystrophy (PPMD)*, we completed the necessary arrangements. Despite the three-hour journey to Billings, Montana, we were undeterred. During our visit to Dr. Wiggins' office, he concurred with the treatment plan, recommending beta blockers and ace inhibitors for Riley. Our relentless advocacy for Riley paid off, averting potential crises.

Between ages 10 and 14, we maintained regular appointments with Dr. Wiggins every six months and returned to *Cincinnati Children's Hospital* annually for comprehensive evaluations by the *DMD* specialists. Fortunately, Riley's progress was positive, with excellent checkups indicating that the beta blockers and ace inhibitors were effectively managing his condition.

As Ron's mother used to say, "If Life is a Bowl of Cherries, What Am I Doing in the Pits?!" This book title by author Erma Bombeck resonates with us during the tumultuous times in our lives.[15] Often, it feels like we're stuck in the pits. Our approach has always been to prepare for the worst while hoping for the best. Every right or wrong decision has been made with Riley's best interests at heart. With Dr. Wiggin's assistance and the steadfast support from our *DMD* family, we managed to emerge from the pits and savor some cherries for a brief respite.

Friendships and DMD

"It seems they had always been, and always would be, friends. Time could change, but not that."[16]

When Riley and Lexi were young, we had two sets of friends from the beginning. It would be remiss of me not to include them in Riley's story because they played a significant role in our lives. As they were growing up, Riley experienced an upbringing in what could only be described as an idyllic environment. A big part of this idyllic life was due to the presence of our dear friends and their children, who treated Riley and Lexi as their own family.

Our cherished friends, Deb and Roc Apple, and their children, Cody and Jessie, were integral to our lives. Our friendship with the Apples began when we lived in our first home in Helena, Montana, at Ten Mile Creek Estates. We instantly hit it off, and the kids loved spending time together. Cody was Riley's best friend.

Similarly, Eileen and Joe Mueller and their children - Jack, Lee, Maddy, Joe, and Sarah - were also dear to us. My bond with the Mueller family began when I taught Eileen's eldest son at preschool. We quickly became close friends, and the children also formed strong bonds.

"It was the best of times, the worst of times."[17] This description encapsulates our relationship with Deb and Roc Apple. From the days when our kids were in grade school all the way through middle school, high school, college, and beyond, we could always depend on them. In times of joy and sorrow, they were steadfast allies, offering comfort and support when tragedy touched our lives. Their presence was a source of great solace to my mother, father, and Lexi when they needed it most.

Raising a child with *DMD* can be isolating, and one must learn to cultivate strong friendships and trust that they will embrace both you and the challenges that come with *DMD*. Fortunately, these friends immediately embraced Riley's disability without hesitation. They treated him no differently, and their children followed suit. This unconditional acceptance was what I valued most about them. Their steadfast companionship and affection would shape Riley's childhood in profound ways. We shared countless summers together -- boating, playing on the beach, and enjoying evenings at Ron's family cabin. We treasured These moments deeply, always mindful of the reality that Riley's circumstances could shift suddenly.

Friendships are constantly evolving. As time passes, our schedules have become more hectic, making it harder to find time to be together. However, this does not diminish the importance of our friendships. We have shared some truly special moments, and I will always cherish the kindness and generosity shown by our friends. While friendships may come and go, the memories created will last a lifetime.

Although Riley can no longer join in the activities and antics we once enjoyed with our group of friends, we still fondly reminisce about earlier times. These shared memories never fail to bring a smile to our faces, and often belly laughs. Some people are only meant to be part of our lives briefly, while others stay longer. We have come to appreciate these experiences and treasure our many adventures together.

One friendship that still holds strong is with my friend Heidi Blossom and her husband, Mick. I first met Heidi at *Early Movement Preschool* when I taught her two boys, Bryce and Reese. Her magnetic personality and medical knowledge (as a nurse) have always astounded me. She has been with me through thick and thin, always there to calm my fears and neurotic tendencies regarding Riley's care. Heidi has never hesitated to come at a moment's notice when Riley felt sick. Her expertise as a nurse and prior understanding of Riley's condition has been incredibly valuable, providing me with excellent advice through numerous episodes.

Heidi's husband, Mick, is a charismatic and fun-loving individual. He is the kind of person who will drop everything to lend a helping hand. For instance, who else would build a ramp so Riley could access their house, ensuring we didn't spend Christmas Eve alone? Mick, that's who! I have always believed that surrounding oneself with like-minded, kind-hearted individuals is the key to a fulfilling life. We are and always will be deeply appreciative of their friendship.

I also want to mention Stacey Smith, my carpool buddy from the time our kids started elementary school through high school. Her incredible care and attention to Riley and Lexi truly meant the world to me. Our car rides home were never dull, thanks to the fun atmosphere created by Stacey and her three daughters, Madison, Meredith, and Riley

Our bond grew even stronger because we both understood the challenges that come with having a child with heart complications, as her daughter Riley had experienced since infancy. Finding someone who truly comprehended what we were going through provided immeasurable comfort during those difficult times. I always knew that I could count on Stacey for anything, no matter the circumstances.

Good friends are hard to come by, but keeping them is even harder. I would like to give a special thanks to Riley's friends: Coltan Pipinich, Adam Hogan, Logan Cain, Clint Retz, and Brian Retz. Thank you for sticking by him from first grade through high school and beyond. The greatest gift you gave him was making him feel like he was one of the guys, not just someone with a terminal disease.

As we get older, people and lives change, but you can never take away the fond memories we built together that were such a vital part of our children's childhood. We wouldn't take one second back of any of it. Thanks for the memories!

Middle School Blues

We often wonder how we can support Riley in enhancing his quality of life. Mental well-being is crucial and should be taken into account when your child is dealing with a life-threatening illness.

Transitioning children from elementary to middle school can be challenging for parents, often referred to as the "middle school blues." Many parents can relate to this sentiment. Whether your child is thriving or facing challenges, it's natural to have concerns about their social integration, academic performance, and overall adjustment to a new school environment. This period marks a significant transition for your tween, and adjusting to these changes can be daunting.

By the time Riley entered middle school, Ron and I were finely attuned to his needs. Yet, a lingering sense of uncertainty persisted regarding how Riley would adapt and whether his condition would progress unexpectedly. At times, it felt like plummeting into an abyss. Before starting the school year, I had already visited *C.R. Anderson*, Riley's middle school, to kick-start preparations. The more information I could furnish them, the greater the chances of Riley having a successful academic year.

Despite our concerns about Riley's transition, we deemed it prudent to seek the assistance of a psychologist. Our aim was to ensure Riley felt comfortable discussing his fears, anxieties, and challenges arising from this significant change. This would also provide him with an additional outlet to express himself beyond our conversations. Riley saw this therapist throughout the first two years of middle school. He managed to maintain his existing friendships from elementary school while forging new ones along the way. He navigated these relationships adeptly, and his experience at *C.R. Anderson* surpassed our expectations.

Throughout his time at *C.R. Anderson*, Riley remained on his heart medication and had regular appointments with Dr. Wiggins, in addition to yearly check-ups at *CCH*. We were overjoyed and grateful for the positive experiences during those initial two years.

As Riley embarked on his final year, eighth grade at *C.R. Anderson*, he remained remarkably high functioning for a teenager with *DMD*.

Excitement brimmed within him as he anticipated the role of an upperclassman. The summer preceding this milestone was filled with joy, spent boating on the lake with family and friends. Riley could still leap off the back of the boat, swim to the ladder, and receive a boost from Ron. Tubing with Lexi was another highlight, with many of his middle school friends joining in on the fun at the lake. It was a summer of happiness for all of us.

Amidst boating escapades and July barbecues, we returned to *Cincinnati Children's Hospital* for Riley's annual check-up. This visit included his first cardiac *MRI*, a moment of excitement and trepidation. We trusted his heart medications' efficacy and hoped for positive results. Following a week of consultations and tests at *CCH*, the cardiac *MRI* results arrived, keeping us on tenterhooks. The news was reassuring – Riley's heart had shown improvement since his last appointment with Dr. Wiggins in Billings, MT. The medical team commended our efforts and Riley's progress, expressing satisfaction with the results. With renewed gratitude and a sense of peace, we returned to Montana, having overcome yet another hurdle in Riley's battle with *DMD*. Our exceptional care team in Cincinnati, led by the remarkable Pat Furlong, once again guided us through another obstacle. We had successfully kept "The Beast" at bay, allowing us to breathe a collective sigh of relief.

A Nick Here, A Nick There...

At present, the severe noncardiac manifestations of *DMD* prevent the majority of *DMD* patients from being viable candidates for a heart transplant. However, if new therapies could mitigate the noncardiac morbidity and mortality in this population, heart transplantation could potentially become a more realistic option.

In the fall, Riley began eighth grade without any issues. However, as the next few months passed, we started to notice a change in Riley's energy levels. He would come home more exhausted than usual and struggling more physically. Around this time, Ron contacted the Montana Hope Project, who generously offered to sponsor a trip to New York for Riley. Both Riley and Lexi were infatuated with the idea of visiting New

York during Christmas time - seeing the Rockefeller Christmas tree, taking a carriage ride in Central Park, watching a Broadway show, and exploring the *American Museum of Natural History*. Riley's wish was granted, and we set off for New York in December 2006 for the Christmas break. The trip was truly magical, but not without some bumps along the way. The hustle and bustle of New York proved to be tiring and overwhelming, even for those with high stamina. We felt sluggish in the first few days before we acclimated to the pace. It became apparent that Riley was having difficulty keeping up with the rest of us during the trip.

Quoting Arthur Ashe, "A nick here, a nick there, and pretty soon you're bleeding to death."[18]

Unfortunately, this was not the only time Riley faced such formidable obstacles. He was fatigued from the beginning, and his get–up–and–go had, gotten-up-and–went! Ron began carrying Riley during long walks in New York. Ron became hyper-aware of his increasing paleness, as his skin had a grayish tinge. Riley's successful checkup in July led us to quickly shift our focus away from his heart. Instead, we were more laser-focused on the idea that Riley was progressing physically with his *DMD*.

Our main goal was to ensure that the rest of the vacation was as enjoyable as possible. Ron continued to carry Riley whenever necessary for the remainder of the trip. Experiencing New York City during the holiday season was as enchanting as possible, and Riley and Lexi were tickled pink to have had this magical experience.

Coming home after such an exhilarating time, we understood the importance of allowing Riley to readjust to his regular routine. He spent the remainder of the Christmas break unwinding, and we made a point to keep a close eye on him. With Riley's upcoming heart appointment scheduled for January, we felt reassured knowing we could discuss any concerns with Dr. Wiggins.

January 15, 2007, Changed Our Lives Forever

Heading to Billings, MT, for his heart checkup, we didn't anticipate any red flags would indicate something was amiss with Riley's heart. Ron accompanied Riley while I stayed home with Lexi, assuming it was a routine follow-up appointment. Our primary concern was his physical development. We viewed this appointment as a mere formality; another *EKG* and echocardiogram would be conducted. We expected Dr. Wiggins to reassure Ron and Riley that everything appeared fine and to continue as planned.

Ron called me after the appointment with Dr. Wiggins had ended, assuring me that everything had gone well. He and Riley were leaving directly from the office and would be home as soon as possible. The next call I received was from Dr. Wiggins himself. Little did I know this conversation would alter our lives indefinitely.

I remember gazing out the window as Dr. Wiggins delivered the harsh reality about Riley's heart. He chose not to go over the specific test results with Ron in the office, mindful of their lengthy 3-to-4 hour drive ahead. He didn't want Ron to be at risk of an accident due to being preoccupied with the impending news he was about to share with me. A tear welled up in my eye, and I felt a sense of numbness wash over my entire body.

Riley's heart was failing; he had cardiomyopathy secondary to *DMD*, or in other terms, *Dilated Cardiomyopathy*. He was in the final stages of complete heart failure, as his heart was no longer functioning properly. The only solution would be for him to undergo a heart transplant.

Montana is a state with limited resources and was unable to facilitate a heart transplant. The best that Dr. Wiggins could do was to help us make Riley feel comfortable, and in the next few months, he would die. The only viable solution was to consider relocating to another state where Riley could undergo a life-saving heart transplant. Dr. Wiggins assured me of his support and urged me to take the time to consider our options before making a decision. His compassionate tone reflected the difficulty of delivering such devastating news, especially considering the emotional weight of the situation as I faced it alone. Dr. Wiggins demonstrated his dedication to his patients through his kindness, empathy, and genuine concern for Riley's well-being.

After hanging up the phone, the agonizing silence was almost deafening. I closed my eyes and heard myself screaming, "Why, God, why? After all he's been through, he doesn't deserve any of this." I opened my eyes and realized it was all in my head. I was left staring at the ceiling when the floodgates opened, and I was sobbing uncontrollably in complete shock.

I had to endure three torturous hours alone with nothing but my thoughts. I can't even remember how I managed to get through it. I was acutely aware that I couldn't reach out to anyone else before informing Ron. Lexi was away at a friend's place, and I didn't want her to witness me in the depths of despair, shock, and hopelessness. The whole experience seemed like a blur. All I can remember is feeling as if I was trapped in a fog, with our entire life together flashing before my eyes as I pondered what the future held. It was undeniably one of the loneliest times I have ever felt in my life. Riley's fate hung precariously in the balance.

How was I going to break this news to Ron? Then, we would have to figure out how to discuss this with Riley. My God, he is only 14 years old; how will he deal with another blow at such a young age? Up to this point, we had experienced many life-changing moments in our brief history with Riley, but this soul-crushing news had to be the hardest of all. I could feel my heart shattering into a million pieces. The one thought that kept haunting me was when Dr. Cripe and Pat Furlong told us that Riley might not be eligible for a heart transplant. His *DMD* may have progressed too far for his body to endure such a major surgery. I replayed that conversation over and over in my mind like a broken record.

Then Ron and Riley walked through the door.

Life is fragile, yet we hold onto it with all our might. Riley is so strong and such a fighter. I knew that whatever was thrown at him, somehow, he would pull through. He was becoming good at proving everybody wrong. Why should this time be any different? It is unbelievable to me the strength, absolute power, and will to live this son of mine possesses. He has already lived a lifetime in his 14 years on this earth.

When it comes to "The Beast," that is *DMD*, you must care for your sons as if your life depended on it because it does! Every day is a fight to have another day. The only way for me to explain it would be that you are constantly in survival mode. The term fight or flight means absolutely nothing. You are in a continuous loop of fight, fight, and fight!

Catch-22

Having *Duchenne muscular dystrophy* with heart complications is akin to a *Catch-22* situation. *Catch-22* is a dilemma or difficult circumstance without escape because of mutually conflicting or dependent conditions. You're damned if you do, and you're damned if you don't. You're in a difficult position regardless of the choices you make. In this instance, it seemed as though we were trapped. We attributed his weakness to the numerous complications linked to *DMD* without considering that it could be related to his heart.

Ron immediately sensed something was amiss when he entered the room with Riley. We retreated to another room, leaving Riley to watch TV in his own space. I broke the difficult news to Ron, observing his reaction unfold like a slow-motion train wreck, inevitable yet impossible to halt. Struggling to find words, we both succumbed to tears. After consoling each other for what felt like an eternity, we knew it was time to break the news to Riley. We approached the task delicately, mindful of his young age and tender emotions.

Shortly after Lexi returned from a friend's house, we decided to deliver the news together to soften the blow. Seated together, we gently began to share the news with them. Surprisingly, Riley received the news with remarkable composure, his innate ability to remain calm under pressure shining through. In contrast, Lexi's tears flowed freely as she empathized with her older brother's plight. Following a moment of emotional release, Riley gathered his thoughts and asked, "You're going to help me get a new heart, right?" We assured him we would spare no effort in seeking a solution. Riley's unbelievable faith in our ability to explore solutions together has been a source of strength for us all as we maneuver the complexities of living with DMD.

Now is the Time

Keeping the Faith

I called my parents when I finished updating Ron on Riley's recent heart checkup. I picked up the phone, dialed their number, and my mom answered first. I asked her to pass the phone to Dad so they could both hear the news at the same time. They were eager to hear about Riley's appointment in Billings. We always kept my parents in the loop, so they were expecting the call. My mom was my rock, someone I could confide in and seek motherly advice from.

Their initial reaction to the news of Riley's failing heart mirrored our shock and dismay. I never broached the topic of my mom's emotional struggle upon learning about Riley's diagnosis; it seemed too painful for her to revisit. The wound ran deep, and I didn't want to reopen it. My mom always felt the need to be strong, which sometimes led others to perceive her as stern, but we kids knew better.

Later on, my mom shared her experience upon learning about Riley's *DMD* diagnosis for the first time. She had lost faith, felt hopeless, and descended into a dark period, even renouncing her religion. She grappled with feelings of isolation and depression, putting on a brave face whenever I was around. I was completely unaware of her inner turmoil. Despite wanting to reach out, she struggled to find the strength.

As the youngest child, I shared a close bond with my mom. She was a dedicated parent, attending all my activities and events, embodying the quintessential stay-at-home mom. Seeing how Ron and I handled Riley's situation thus far reassured her we could handle any hardships ahead, despite their magnitude. Witnessing our love, faith, and hope for Riley reignited her own faith. Her unrelenting belief in Ron and me was a testament to the strength of her love and hope. I miss her dearly, and her acknowledgment of our resilience in the face of adversity remains one of the most profound things she has ever shared with me. Her absolute faith in us was a powerful source of strength, rooted in the love and hope she witnessed firsthand.

Through the years, I have found comfort and solace in those words. With each revelation, I have always known that I could turn to her for anything. On my toughest days, when tears would flow, she would cry alongside me, offering unyielding support. During moments of joy, she stood by me, cheering me on from the sidelines. Her profound insight into my identity has been a steadfast source of strength and motivation.

The next phone call we made was to Greg and Dave. They had been with us every step of the way. Their immediate response was, "How can we help?" Despite their devastation, they reassured us that Riley was in good hands and expressed full confidence in us. I recall them saying, "If anyone can pull this off, it's the two of you." We proceeded to contact our family and friends to share details of the situation.

The most significant accomplishment in your life should not be defined by your job, income, property ownership, or social circle; rather, it should be your children. Your pursuit of success should be driven by the desire to provide for your children, enabling them to thrive and develop in a secure, nurturing environment. Right now, our greatest achievement has yet to be determined. In anticipation of what lay ahead, we turned to Pat Furlong for guidance.

The looming presence of "The Beast" lingered in our thoughts because we knew it wouldn't be long before it reared its ugly head again. Our fears materialized as Riley's aging heart managed to endure four years under the care and medication regimen prescribed by Dr. Wiggins.

Don't Judge a Book by It's Cover (Quality of Life)

Stephen Hawking vs. LeBron James or Brain vs. Braun

When considering quality of life, how can one even begin to compare? I often ponder these two remarkable individuals as prime examples of this complex issue, with Riley holding them both in the highest esteem.

Is LeBron James' quality of life truly superior to that of Stephen Hawking? It's akin to attempting to scale Mt. Everest without a safety rope. How can one juxtapose the most brilliant mind on the planet with the finest athlete? Who are we to determine whose societal contributions hold more weight?

For instance, Stephen Hawking's groundbreaking scientific revelations have fundamentally altered our understanding of the universe. Despite being confined to a wheelchair and unable to speak unaided, he managed to make these extraordinary contributions. On the other hand, we have the iconic LeBron James, whose impact on the sport of basketball and philanthropic endeavors to assist the less fortunate are truly remarkable. How can a decision be made?

One cannot simply prioritize individuals like Stephen Hawking over LeBron James on a transplant list based on perceived quality of life. Both must be afforded equal opportunities.

I often refer to this comparison as it resonates with many due to the widespread recognition of these two distinguished men. While they may appear to be at opposite ends of the spectrum, it is imperative that both are given a fair chance. It is not a matter of choosing between Hawking and James; rather, it is about providing both an opportunity to excel and witnessing the incredible outcomes that may result.

The potential accomplishments and groundbreaking discoveries that individuals with *DMD* can achieve may never be fully known. Their resilience is extraordinary, and they deserve the chance to thrive and make their mark in this world!

Where Can He Get a Transplant?

"The Last Best Place" is an affectionate description of Montana, a state many proudly call home. However, Montana may not be the ideal location for individuals facing serious medical conditions such as *Duchenne muscular dystrophy* or in need of a heart transplant.

I had already navigated the joys and challenges of living in Montana when my parents were trying to determine what was ailing Greg and Dave. The nightmare repeated itself when Riley was diagnosed. While I cherished my upbringing in Montana and considered myself fortunate to raise my children there with my husband Ron, accessing the necessary care was undeniably a struggle. When Montana proved unable to meet Riley's medical needs, Pat Furlong, *PPMD*, and *CCH* stepped in to help.

Upon learning of Riley's failing heart from Dr. Wiggins, my husband and I immediately reached out to Pat Furlong. She shared our disbelief and recommended Cincinnati Children's Hospital *(CCH)*, as the best place for Riley's heart transplant. Given our desire to remain close to Montana and family, we explored the possibility of Riley receiving treatment in a neighboring state. Although *CCH* was 1,800 miles away from us and far from our loved ones, we considered options in Salt Lake City (500 miles away) and Denver (800 miles away) as well. Pat Furlong and Dr. Cripe facilitated discussions with these institutions, emphasizing the urgency of our decision due to the time-sensitive nature of Riley's condition.

Our initial contact with the transplant team in Salt Lake City was met with reluctance and concerns about transplanting a *DMD* patient for the first time, raising quality-of-life considerations. Frustrated by their hesitance, we quickly realized that Salt Lake City might not fit Riley well. Similarly, our interactions with the team in Denver revealed uncertainties about prioritizing Riley on the transplant waiting list, leading to doubts about their commitment to his case. The notion of potentially being bumped down the list based on perceived quality-of-life criteria was unacceptable to us. Nobody is going to tell me my son's life isn't worth fighting for. NOBODY!

Feeling increasingly cornered by these setbacks, we refused to be deterred by the discrimination and prejudice we encountered while seeking treatment for Riley. Our resolve to fight for his life only strengthened our conviction that *CCH* was the most suitable place for his life-saving procedure. With Pat Furlong and Dr. Cripe's staunch support, we made the decision to proceed with *Cincinnati Children's Hospital*.

As we prepared for Riley's journey to *CCH* for testing and placement on the transplant waiting list, we encountered another obstacle when Dr. Wiggins advised against commercial air travel for Riley. Instead, he would need to be life-flighted from our local hospital in Helena, MT, to

Cincinnati. Dr. Wiggins delivered the difficult news to us on Monday. By Tuesday, we made the decision to proceed with *CCH*, and by Wednesday, Riley was admitted to St. Peter's to be airlifted.

Ron and I were granted permission to fly to Cincinnati on the Learjet with Riley. He was transported by ambulance to the airport and then onto the plane, lying on a medical bed connected to numerous machines.

Our entire family gathered at the hospital to bid Riley farewell. It was an incredibly emotional moment for all of us. we were venturing into uncharted territory; all we could do was pray and place our trust in *CCH*, Parent Project Muscular Dysrophy (*PPMD)*, and Pat Furlong.

Medical staff had to monitor Riley's vitals throughout the journey to ensure his well-being. Boarding the small aircraft with the medical team was nerve-wracking. Ron and I clung to each other during the flight, praying for the best possible outcome.

Initially, Riley would need to meet all criteria for the transplant. This involved a series of tests to confirm his suitability as a candidate for a new heart. He would undergo a week-long admission to the hospital for evaluation. The *Cincinnati Children's Hospital* (*CCH*) team expressed full confidence that Riley would successfully clear all their assessments.

Recognizing the complexity of the situation, we planned for Lexi's care with my parents while we focused on Riley's treatment. Understanding the situation well, Lexi shared her fears and hopes for Riley. Witnessing Riley's physical condition was particularly difficult for her.

If Riley were to require a lung and heart transplant, his weakened body wouldn't be able to withstand the procedure due to his *DMD*. In such a scenario, bringing him home to spend his final days seemed inevitable.

Cincinnati Children's Hospital (*CCH*) provided us with the support and resources needed to face this daunting challenge. Given the considerable distance from our small town of Helena, MT, Cincinnati seemed like a world away. Both *CCH* and *Parent Project Muscular Dystrophy* (*PPMD*) remained committed in their determination to make this transplant a reality. We placed our trust in the individuals who believed in

Riley's potential. While it may sound repetitive, the upcoming week promised to be one of the most arduous trials we had ever faced.

Despite the uncertainty, our unfaltering determination and the support of *CCH*, *PPMD*, and Pat Furlong fueled our hope for Riley's recovery, guiding us through the difficult decisions that lie ahead.

One of the tests that assessed his respiratory function was spirometry, which is commonly requested by doctors. The typical combination of tests requested by doctors includes spirometry (both before and after using bronchodilators), gas transfer assessment, and lung volume measurement. Spirometry evaluates the volume and speed of air that can be forcefully exhaled from the lungs after taking a deep breath.

Another test Riley had to undergo was the lung function test. When Riley was younger, we enrolled him in swimming lessons to help develop his lung capacity. Boys with *DMD* often experience lung and respiratory issues as the disease progresses. Riley's swim instructor focused on breathing techniques and monitored how long he could hold his breath underwater. It was crucial to strengthen these functions to support his overall health. We continued the lessons until he started Middle School. Eventually, we had to discontinue them when he faced challenges getting out of the pool and refused assistance. Nevertheless, the swimming lessons significantly improved his respiratory and lung functions. When the time came to assess his need for a lung transplant, he passed the test with flying colors. Our past efforts had paid off tenfold. We were truly grateful for the positive outcome. Thank God!

With this disease, someone needed to step up and stop saying "NO" and start saying "YES." That person, for us, was Pat Furlong. Pat always had a unique perspective on how things should unfold. She looked at all these boys and consistently responded with a resounding "Yes" to ensure they had a fighting chance. Pat was intimately familiar with this situation because her two incredible boys succumbed to *DMD* at a tragically young age.

She urged us to approach Riley's life-and-death situation in the simplest manner possible to help him maintain a positive outlook. She advised against divulging all the potential negative outcomes, as that would only weigh him down. We have always believed knowledge is crucial but should be delivered in small, manageable doses. We placed our trust in her guidance because we knew that everything she shared with us was in Riley's best interest. We leaned on her heavily, and she stood by us every step of the way.

Going Home to Say Goodbye

Our next step in the journey was to return to Helena, pack our bags, sort out our finances, bid farewell to our loved ones, and make our way back to Cincinnati, where we held onto hope and prayer for Riley's timely heart transplant. Before our departure, Riley underwent a procedure to sustain his failing heart until the arrival of the new one. A *PICC* line was inserted at the hospital and connected to a small portable pump, delivering essential intravenous medications such as *milrinone* to his heart. This temporary measure served as a stopgap until Riley could receive his new heart, requiring him to carry the heart pump in a bag slung over his shoulder. At least we could fly home on a commercial airline.

We were eager to return home and organize everything for the move. Uncertain about how long we would be in Cincinnati, we felt compelled to make the move for Riley's health.

The situation placed a significant burden on our family, both emotionally and financially. Relocating to Cincinnati was necessary for Riley's transplant and the essential post-operative care. *Parent Project Muscular Dystrophy* (*PPMD*) generously arranged an apartment for us in Hyde Park. Proximity to the hospital was crucial, requiring us to be within a 15–20-minute drive. We were immensely grateful for the support, knowing we didn't have to face this challenge alone.

Upon our return from Cincinnati, the sight of Lexi and my parents brought us immense joy. They shared our anxiety and relief. Tears welled up in Lexi's and my mom's eyes as they laid eyes on Riley while my dad struggled to hold back his emotions, his voice breaking as he spoke. It was a deeply emotional reunion for all of us.

The following day was a school day, and Riley was eager to attend despite the circumstances. He insisted on going, even though he had to carry the cumbersome heart pump with him, holding it like a purse. Physically weak, he struggled with the weight of it all. The doctors had advised him against going to school, but skipping school was out of the question for Riley as it held significant importance in his life. Being in middle school was his lifeline, his reason to push forward. The doctors warned him to head home if he felt tired to avoid exerting unnecessary energy.

Each morning, I would drop him off at school, tears welling up in my eyes as he walked in with determination. He made it through to lunch with his friends, only for me to receive the call to pick him up later in the day. His frailty prevented him from enduring the full school day. This routine persisted for the next two weeks until we relocated to Cincinnati. While most kids might opt to stay home due to embarrassment, fatigue, or sheer reluctance, Riley was different. As a dedicated student, the school held the utmost importance for him.

During this brief period, our schedule was packed. I returned to my cherished preschool, where I was warmly welcomed by all. By now, all the parents at the preschool were aware of my circumstances. Normally private about my personal life, I typically focused my attention on the preschool during my time there. The parents entrusted their children to *Early Movement Preschool*, expecting my full dedication.

Teaching brought me immense joy, knowing I could create a safe, stimulating environment for the children to explore, learn, and express themselves freely. I informed everyone of my upcoming leave of absence, ensuring them that my capable staff would take over. Many parent volunteers were delighted to fill in the gap when called upon. I would remain in constant communication with the teachers daily and be involved in the administrative aspects. *Early Movement Preschool* was my pride and joy, and I wanted to keep my reputation intact.

Ron's workplace understood his situation and allowed him to work remotely. They also connected him with the Cincinnati field office, enabling him to stay employed. He refrained from taking vacation days, knowing they would be crucial after Riley's transplant.

Meanwhile, amidst the chaos, my parents made their own arrangements. They closed their house in Butte, Montana, and relocated 63 miles away to our home, ensuring Lexi could maintain a sense of normalcy without too much upheaval. The stability of living in her home and being cared for by her grandparents while she attended school was much more appealing than staying elsewhere. She needed this routine to focus on her studies with minimal disruptions. Lexi and my parents would need to put in a substantial amount of effort, but I had faith they could handle it. I trusted that my parents would provide excellent care for her, and I hoped that Lexi would be able to persevere through it all. Our family had never been separated for such an extended period. And I agonized over leaving her behind. However, I knew it was the best decision, and I could only hope she would understand.

It's Not Easy Being a Mother

It's not easy being a mother. If it were easy, fathers would do it. I must say, most of the time, this statement rings true. My mom always said, "A mother does what she has to do to get things done."

In times of trouble, and being the strong Catholic she was, my mother would often say, "Nina, we all have our crosses to bear; it's how we carry them that define us." Her words never failed to comfort me whenever I found myself at a crossroads. As I faced the upcoming turn of events, I knew that my mother's wisdom would prove invaluable once again.

It was just over a week before our departure, and things were incredibly tense at the Herrera household. I was juggling taking Lexi and Riley to school and teaching at the preschool until I had to pick up Riley. Then, it was back to preschool to finish the day and collect Lexi for her basketball practice. On one day, it was time to get Riley into the bathtub after returning home. Due to his *PICC* line, he couldn't shower, so I assisted him with his bath. As Riley was in the tub, the phone rang. Lexi's basketball coach was on the line, informing me that Lexi had been injured during practice and needed immediate attention at the emergency room. He refrained from providing details over the phone to prevent upsetting Lexi before my arrival.

I quickly contacted Ron at his workplace, instructing him to come home at once to look after Riley. After explaining the situation to Riley, I left him in the bathtub and hurried to the practice venue. Upon arrival, I found Lexi with ice-wrapped wrists, crying in agony. The coach informed me that he suspected both wrists were broken, leaving me stunned and skeptical.

The timing couldn't have been worse, just a week before our departure. I thought I was going to lose my mind! I rushed Lexi to the *ER*, where it was confirmed that both wrists were indeed fractured. She was doing running drills and was supposed to run to the line, touch it, and run back backward. She tripped and tried to catch herself on her way back when both wrists snapped.

Following a three-hour wait, she returned home wearing casts, needing to keep them on for 4-6 weeks. Ron was shocked and disbelieving at the unfortunate turn of events. Lexi was unable to do anything for herself. The poor girl couldn't even use the bathroom without assistance. Her struggles extended to simple tasks like brushing her teeth, getting dressed, and feeding herself, creating endless challenges. On one hand, we had a child who was dying and needed life-saving surgery, and the other child couldn't even do the most menial tasks. What was a mother to do? I picked myself up, dusted myself off, and did what I had to do to get things done! Thanks for the pep talk, Mom.

Being at home during that final week was a whirlwind. I found myself battling to take Riley and Lexi to school while preparing my preschool for my upcoming leave of absence and getting us ready to leave for Cincinnati. The stress was mounting as Ron and I were like two ships passing in the night. We were barely managing to keep it together. It seemed like God was preparing us for the rigorous road ahead.

Things started falling into place in the last two days, and I began to feel more at ease about our impending departure. However, life takes an unexpected sharp left turn when you least expect it.

Lexi, who was in seventh grade at the time, was facing the typical challenges of middle school on top of dealing with some personal issues. It was unfathomable for her to comprehend what was taking place. Emotions were running high in our family, and tensions were taking their toll on all of us.

Lexi was still supporting the basketball team from the sidelines. After picking her up from practice, I thought she was starting to come to terms with our leaving. But her reaction indicated otherwise. She expressed her sadness and fear about us leaving, especially worrying about being left with her grandparents, whom she affectionately referred to as Nanny and Papa.

Our conversation took a heartbreaking turn when she tearfully expressed her concerns, stating, "Mom, how can you leave me here with two broken wrists? Nanny and Papa don't know how to take care of me. I can't believe you're leaving me behind."

I could hear the panic in her voice, which stirred up a whirlwind of emotions within me. Tears welled up in my eyes as we pulled into the driveway. Gathering my thoughts, I finally spoke, "You know how much I love you, but your brother is fighting for his life. Do you want him to lose this battle?"

Her response was barely audible, "No."

"Then I must go to Cincinnati to do everything in my power to save his life. I have to choose him right now. Just like I would choose you if you were in his place. You will be in the loving care of Nanny and Papa. They will guide you through this strenuous time. I trust them with all my heart to look after you."

I knew that my decision was breaking her heart, but I could see in her eyes that she comprehended the gravity of the situation. We simply couldn't divide our attention between Lexi and Riley. Our conflicting emotions were overwhelming, especially for her, as the fear of losing Riley loomed over us all.

That night, as I lay in bed, tears streaming down my face, I prayed fervently. Both of my children were enduring unimaginable pain. "Please, God, grant me strength. We are making sacrifices because we believe Riley's life is worth fighting for. Please let our efforts not be in vain."

The day we departed for Cincinnati, our family and friends gathered at the airport to bid us goodbye. It was a bittersweet moment. As we prepared to go through security and begin our journey, unexpected events unfolded. Lexi stood there, bravely waving farewell despite her two broken wrists, tears rolling down her cheeks. Then, it was Riley's turn to pass through security, but it didn't go smoothly for us. Riley was stopped by a *TSA* agent and subjected to a pat-down. The agent insisted that Riley remove his *PICC* line, a request that left both Riley and I bewildered. We tried to explain that the *PICC* line was surgically implanted and couldn't be removed, but our explanations fell on deaf ears, causing a delay in the line. Eventually, the head of security intervened, examined the device, and granted us passage. Looking back, we often chuckle at this absurd incident.

While in Cincinnati, we needed a car, as well as clothing and other essentials. Ron took on the responsibility of driving to Cincinnati, and Riley and I planned to meet him there. Our whole life was carefully packed into the Toyota Camry. Ron bid us farewell at the Helena airport before embarking on the long journey to Cincinnati.

Waiting for a New Heart

Don't judge Riley based on his disability; instead, judge him based on his abilities.

Duchenne muscular dystrophy (*DMD*) was a significant factor throughout the transplant process, as it was the primary reason for his need for the transplant. Given that the heart is a muscle that contains *dystrophin*, a deficiency in this protein results in muscle degeneration in the heart. We were informed that less than 4% of children with *DMD* experience severe *cardiomyopathy* that necessitates a heart transplant. Riley was in the lucky 4%. We seem to have bad luck once again.

When we arrived in Cincinnati, Riley had a series of appointments to ensure everything was proceeding according to plan. One crucial milestone was meeting with a review board to obtain approval for the transplant. We underwent interviews to assess our ability to care for Riley post-transplant. They needed to determine if we were capable of the task. At one stage, they interviewed us individually. It was stressful as we were confident in our ability to care for him, but we had to persuade them. Fortunately, we received approval! This was one step closer to achieving our ultimate goal.

My mother's mantra was, "Normalcy, Normalcy, Normalcy." She emphasized striving for it every day and making it a priority. My parents ingrained in me the importance of living a regular life.

"When life gives you lemons, make lemonade." It felt like we were constantly making lemonade every step of the way. Although waiting for a heart transplant didn't deter Riley from completing the eighth grade, his focus remained on progressing through middle school and transitioning to high school alongside his peers. After connecting with *C.R. Anderson Junior High School*, his teachers and administrators approved my role as his tutor. Transitioning from teaching preschool children to tutoring Riley became my new focus until the transplant. I always had my teacher's hat on.

The hospital had provided Ron and I with a set of beepers. They served as our lifeline, and we had to have them with us 24/7 in case a donor's heart was located for Riley. Additionally, we had to always be within a 15-20-minute radius of the hospital.

Riley's time in Cincinnati wasn't all doom and gloom. We also experienced some lighthearted moments as we endeavored to maintain a sense of normalcy. Riley has always had a passion for food and considers himself somewhat of a foodie. We allowed him to choose a restaurant one evening as a special treat. To our surprise, he selected a fancy Italian restaurant for our dining experience.

Being unfamiliar with the workings of a big city, we struggled with the complexities of the parking situation near the restaurant. Ultimately, we parked in a lot adjacent to a fast-food establishment. Upon entering the Italian restaurant, we were promptly seated. However, our attention was soon diverted as we glanced out the window only to witness a tow truck beginning to tow away our car, sending us into a state of panic. Our car was essential in case our beepers went off. In a frantic effort to resolve the situation, Ron ran outside and hastily engaged in a heated discussion with the tow truck driver. When he came back inside, he exclaimed, "Nina, give me all the cash you have. I need to pay a bribe to rescue our car." Scrounging together a total of $80, Ron rushed out and handed the money to the driver, who promptly dropped our car on the spot. Looking back, we now chuckle about the incident, but at the moment, it was undeniably a nerve-wracking ordeal. Whew! Another crisis was successfully averted.

Out with the Old, In with the New

Riley always had a unique way of compartmentalizing things. It seemed to be his survival tactic to inject some humor into a serious situation. When he decided it was "out with the old, in with the new," it was time to bid farewell to the old heart and welcome the new one. It was his quirky way of finding some comic relief in the midst of adversity. Unsurprisingly, he even gave names to his old heart and the new one he would soon receive. He affectionately named his old heart Jeffrey while he dubbed his upcoming new heart Eddie. To him, these organs were almost like real beings, each with its own personality. Riley would talk about them as if they were characters in a story. He often joked that Jeffrey had put in a good run, but it was now time for Eddie to step in and take charge.

At the age of 14, Riley was mature enough to grasp the gravity of his situation, yet he retained a youthful resilience that refused to be overshadowed by fear. He placed his trust in the skilled hands of the doctors at *CCH* and the support of individuals like Pat Furlong. Riley eagerly anticipated the arrival of Eddie, viewing it as a new addition to the family. His ability to see things from a unique perspective was a testament to his courage and optimism.

Be Patient, God is Not Finished with Me Yet

Waiting in the condo for a heart was excruciating. When we heard an ambulance, Riley would wake us up, thinking it was coming for him. How disheartening it was to tell him this wasn't the one. The disappointment at times was unbearable. Each news story about someone injured or involved in an accident would give us false hope that perhaps that day would be the day. It almost felt like we were turning into "ambulance chasers," desperately hoping that the next tragedy might bring the saving grace for our child. This mindset was warped, but it was the reality we were living in. With time, we came to understand that this way of thinking was making us bitter and hardened. We knew we had to step back and see the bigger picture, accepting that "it is what it is!" We needed to move forward with a more positive outlook.

The transplant team at *CCH* was truly incredible! Leading the team were Karen Uzark, the heart transplant coordinator; Dr. Linda Cripe and Dr. Robert Spicer, the Pediatric Cardiologists; Dr. Brenda Wong, the Neurologist; Kathy Kinney, the Nurse Practitioner; and Pat Furlong. They worked tirelessly to ensure Riley received the best possible medical care, and we felt incredibly fortunate and lucky to have such dedicated professionals involved in Riley's care.

It was mid-January when we received the horrific news about Riley's heart, and as March approached, the situation started looking bleak. Riley's condition was deteriorating, and it became clear that having him stay at the condo with us was no longer viable. Consequently, Riley was admitted to *CCH* so he could be monitored more closely until the transplant became possible. At this critical juncture, we were uncertain if he would even survive long enough to undergo the transplant procedure. History has shown us that Riley's body did not tolerate prolonged waiting. When it's time to go, it's all downhill from there. It felt like we were at the cliff's edge, waiting for someone to push us off.

The Preschool Effect

In a close-knit community like Helena, word spread rapidly that Riley was in urgent need of a heart transplant. The preschool staff and parents were deeply aware of the situation and felt compelled to act. Coming together, they reached out to The *Lost & Foundations*[19] and organized a fundraising concert to support Riley and his family. The *Lost and Foundations* was a non-profit organization whose mission was "To raise and distribute financial resources for public health through the power of music."[20] What followed was a remarkable chain of events. Riley's middle school initiated fundraising efforts while friends and family sold raffle tickets, all contributing to the anticipation of an exceptional benefit organized by the non-profit organization.

Ron had a close friend, Steve Sobonya, whom he had met through playing high school football in Helena. Steve, now a renowned strength and conditioning coach for professional athletes worldwide, generously donated boxes of autographed sports memorabilia for the event's auction. Ron's family collaborated with Steve to ensure the merchandise successfully reached the benefit.

aroundthetown

fundraisers

Lost & Foundation

The Lost & Foundation will hold a fundraising concert on Sunday, March 25, at the Red Lion Colonial Hotel from 2 to 10 p.m. Proceeds of the concert will benefit CR Anderson student Riley Herrera and his family.

Herrera, 14, has cardiomyopathy. In January, he was airlifted to intensive care at Cincinnati Children's Hospital, where he and his family learned that he needs a heart transplant. Herrera and his parents, Ron and Nina are living in Cincinnati to be near Children's Hospital while they wait for a transplant to become available. No one knows how long the wait will be. Herrera is doing well but gets tired very easily. He is looking forward to the transplant so he does not have to be tired anymore. After the transplant, he will need another three months of hospital care before coming home.

The Lost & Foundation event will include a huge silent auction featuring art, jewelry, dinners, services, trips and much, much more.

There will also be raffles, 50-50 drawings and other fun activities to help raise funds. The many friends of Herrera's mom Nina, who works at Early Movement Preschool, have organized a wonderful variety of family-oriented activities including pictures with the Easter Bunny, carnival games, play doh making and face painting.

Live music will be performed on three separate stages, where 18 great musical acts, including 9 Miles Up, The MSK Project and The Growlers will donate their time and talents to help the Herrera family.

Other entertainment include a special performance by the Natarajah belly dance troupe.

Lost & Foundation is a nonprofit corporation established by Helena musicians. The group has sponsored several previous concerts and raised over $180,000 for worthy causes. For more information, call 442-5002 or go to www.lostandfoundation.org.

Herrera

www.helenair.com/yt | 05 | Thursday, March 22, 2007

On March 25, 2007, Helena's community rallied together, demonstrating their unwavering support and making the benefit a resounding success. Montana, known as the Treasure State, truly lived up to its name through the generosity and unity displayed by its people. Despite being miles away in Cincinnati, feeling the love and positive energy sent from Helena provided much-needed comfort. As Riley's chances of survival grew slimmer without the transplant, the collective prayers and support from Helena gave us hope during a devastating time.[21]

The dedication and hard work of the preschool parents, staff, family members, and the foundation were truly commendable. They left a lasting impact on us, and they still hold a special place in my heart.

Reader's Alley

Benefit appreciated

On Sunday, March 25, The Lost and Foundation and many, many members of the fine community of Helena came together to host a fundraiser for our son Riley Herrera. Riley is a 14-year-old eighth-grader at CR Anderson. When Riley was 10 years old, he was diagnosed with cardiomyopathy. This past January, we received devastating news that he would need a heart transplant.

Since then we have had to temporarily relocate to Cincinnati so he could receive the transplant. When the Helena community found out about our situation, they jumped right in and contacted the Lost and Foundation to see what could be done to help our family. Many dedicated people volunteered their time and resources to make this extraordiary event possible. We have been so overwhelmed and thankful for all the support we

have received during this difficult time in our lives. We would like to

let everybody know what an amazing place Helena is to live and that we are proud to call it home. Thanks again to the Lost and Foundation and everyone who participated and attended this wonderful benefit to make it such a success. Love,

The Herreras (Ron,
Nina, Lexi and most importantly
Riley)

A Big Thank You!

... to everyone who attended the **Benefit for Riley Herrera** on March 25th at Red Lion Colonial Hotel and Martini's Lounge. You helped raise over $51,000 to help through Riley's heart transplant. Riley received his new heart on March 31, and he is doing well. We also want to thank these **generous merchants & folks for their donations** ...

Carroll College · Mark & Teresa Enger · Jurenka Custom Homes, Inc. · Stephen Locati
One Way Marine · Phalen Ranch · Red Lion Colonial Hotel · Syness Stoneworks

Ron, Riley, Lexi, and I felt so blessed by the outpouring of support of our local community that we wrote a letter to the editor published in the Reader's Alley section of *The Independent Record*, Helena, Montana's local newspaper.

So Close, Yet....So Far!

He who has a why to live for can bear almost any how
--Friedrich Nietzsche

116

Ron and I believed we had addressed all of Riley's physical needs comprehensively, overlooking the potential mental strain it could impose on him. Riley was hospitalized, and we nervously awaited the notification a heart had become available. As we sat by Riley's bedside, we excitedly envisioned the positive outcome of the transplant and all the improvements he would experience. Our optimism was soon overshadowed as "The Beast" resurfaced, this time targeting him emotionally.

Riley's unexpected bombshell admission completely caught us off guard. He bluntly informed us that he had made the decision not to have the transplant. We were shell-shocked. Where had this decision come from? Was he putting on a façade this whole time? He remained resolute in his choice despite our inquiries, providing no explanation. He firmly stated he wasn't having the transplant, and that's that!!

After conferring with Riley's medical team outside his room, we learned that while we couldn't compel him to undergo the transplant, we could attempt to persuade him. Various professionals were brought in to engage with him, yet he remained steadfast in his decision, displaying a defiant attitude. It was a bewildering turn of events at such a watershed moment. How could this be happening at such a crucial time? We were so close, yet so far!

In a final effort to sway Riley, the medical team decided to bring in the big guns. As Catholics, they searched for a priest without success. However, Pastor Bob, known for his impartiality, seemed to fit the bill. We all agreed he was deemed suitable for the task due to his impartial perspective. He proved to be the perfect person for Riley to confide in.

Pastor Bob entered the room and requested that we step out; we strained to listen at the door, and the hallway was silent. After what felt like an eternity but lasted only thirty minutes, Pastor Bob emerged with a broad smile plastered on his face. It was revealed that Riley's apprehension stemmed from not knowing how they would keep him alive during the surgery, as he feared the unknown and the possibility of not surviving. He didn't want to die! He was only 14 years old, and this fear, unbeknownst to anyone, had been the underlying cause of his reluctance. This concept to him was utterly terrifying. One of the doctors entered the room and explained to Riley that he would be connected to a heart-lung bypass machine, which would temporarily take over the functions of his heart and lungs during the transplant procedure.

Riley had always grasped the necessity of the transplant, but he required clarity on the process. His black-and-white thinking demanded concrete answers. With this newfound understanding, the path forward was clear. Full steam ahead and on with the transplant we go.

DMD, *CCH*, and *PPMD*, Oh My!!!

"Challenges make life interesting; however, overcoming them is what makes life meaningful," said Mark Twain.

At this crossroad, we found ourselves powerless over our child's fate, relying solely on hope and prayer for our pleas to be granted.

Dr. Linda Cripe recalls, "When Riley came in, he was very sick and in severe heart failure. I think people had a hard time recognizing how much of his illness was related to his skeletal muscle disease and how much was related to his heart failure. It was easy to attribute most of his problems to his skeletal muscle disease because of his underlying diagnosis of *DMD*. Initially, people didn't want to offer him a heart transplant. It was a tribute to his transplant cardiologist to say, 'No, let's rethink this. You know he's young [he was 14] and will have many years ahead of him. He should not be dying from his *DMD* at age 14. Typically, individuals with those problems have lived into their early 20s. Let's relook at this.'"

Linda continued, "I could easily see and have seen many situations where a similar young man would come in, and he would not be offered a transplant, and instead, he would be sent home or into Hospice care."

Pat said, "Yeah, Linda, I agree with you. I think it is therapeutic nihilism, where this is a skeletal muscle disease. You'll lose all function, so why should we take another step?"

Doctors told us, "We're not prepared to give a transplant to a child with *DMD*." "He would be first on the waiting list now, but in the Spring, we might have one or two others added, so he might not be able to get it."

I asked, "What does that mean?!?!"

118

They responded, "He would go further on down the list."

Linda added, "It's interesting because of an understanding of the challenge described by Pat. Also, *Duchenne's* and *Becker's MD* are essentially the same diseases. One is a milder form than the other, resulting from the same disruption of the same protein molecule, *Dystrophin*. People are a little more willing to transplant individuals with the name *Becker MD* than *Duchenne's MD*, even though they're the same disease. If you don't know much about it, you say they have Becker's, so maybe we'll transplant them. If they have Duchenne's, we won't transplant them. We worked very hard to diagnose him as *Becker MD* instead of *Duchenne*. The neurologist was on board with that. We were stretching the margins to pull this off at the time."

Dr. Robert Spicer, along with Dr. Cripe, was one of the driving forces behind getting Riley his transplant. He truly believed that Riley was the best candidate for this life-saving procedure.

Pat turned to Linda, "Linda, talk about how Riley's health rapidly declined once he got to the hospital."

When she saw Riley's low *EKG*, Linda Cripe (cardiologist) said, "It made my toes curl. I could see Riley's heart beating under his hospital gown. I could see on the monitor that it wasn't the best reporting I'd ever seen. Many times, you know that time was everything for this young man. It was everything for his future."

Waiting for a heart is no small matter, especially when you know that every minute counts. When Riley's heart was at its worst, the weekend of the transplant, Dr. Linda Cripe took pictures of his heart. It was so enlarged she couldn't believe he was still breathing on his own. He had such a powerful will to live.

While all of this was happening, my mom was back at our home in Montana, holding down the fort. Not only was she taking care of Lexi with two broken wrists, but my dad had also suffered a serious fall resulting in a broken hip. He had to stay at a nursing home until he recuperated. Every day, my mom would drop Lexi off at school, visit the nursing home to care for my dad, pick Lexi up after school, and spend time with my dad until dinner. She would then go home, prepare dinner, and tend to Lexi, repeating this routine for two weeks.

I still can't believe how she managed all of this at the age of 73. Even now, as I write about it, I am amazed at her strength and resilience. My mom handled everything with such grace and never let on that she was struggling. She took it upon herself to ensure that everything ran as smoothly as possible.

During this taxing time, my family rallied together to provide my mom with the support and assistance she needed. Greg and Dave made the three-hour round trip from Great Falls to Helena three times a week to visit my dad and check in on my mom and Lexi. My sister, Maria, offered additional support and often picked Lexi up from school. Our friends Deb and Roc also played a crucial role, helping my mom around the house and being frequent visitors at the nursing home while my dad was recovering.

Having family and friends you can rely on during such a formidable time is comforting.

Riley Gets His New Heart

Thursday, March 29, 2007, doctors delivered the devastating news that Riley had just the weekend to receive a heart transplant. They expressed grave concerns that he might not survive the weekend without it. The memory of that conversation is etched in my mind forever. Both Ron and I could see how critical Riley's condition was. He exhibited what is known as the *Death Rattle*, a term indicating the approach of death. It can be described as a distinctive sound that comes from the back of a dying person's throat. It can be characterized by soft, wet, crackling, moan-like snoring or gurgling sounds. This unsettling sound typically signifies that a person has approximately 24 hours to live. Each time Riley coughed, we'd cringe at the sound, and we could see his heart beating out of his chest from underneath his hospital gown. It was a harrowing and distressing sight to behold. Witnessing his struggle TO LIVE, I would have given anything to trade places with him. The profound guilt I experienced as a mother was overwhelming, and I felt as though my heart might cease to beat. While Riley lay motionless in his bed, Ron would steal away for a few moments

120

to the chapel to pray, a ritual he faithfully observed since Riley's admission. In contrast, I grappled with anger, hosting a pity party and questioning why this was happening to us. I recall looking up to the ceiling and screaming silently, asking god, "Why me!" Despite my inner turmoil, I remained resolute in staying by Riley's side, unwilling to leave for fear of missing any precious moments with him, knowing that each one could potentially be our last together.

Friday, March 30, 2007, early morning came, but there was still no heart available for Riley. Family members began calling to inquire about Riley's condition at this point. We informed my brothers that if Riley didn't receive a heart by the weekend, his chances of survival were extremely slim. Riley had been in contact with Greg and Dave daily since our move to Cincinnati. Knowing the seriousness of the situation, they decided they were going to drive through the night to visit him at *CCH*, wanting to bid their final farewells. Nothing was going to stand in their way; they were determined to see Riley one last time. Riley held a special place in their hearts, especially since they did not have children of their own. It was heartbreaking to deliver such gut-wrenching news to them.

Throughout that day, I asked everyone who called to keep Riley in their prayers. We can cling to hope and faith in times like these. It was during this moment that I had a personal epiphany. I guess you could call it my coming to Jesus moment. I went down to the chapel for the first time. I needed a moment alone to gather my thoughts. As I knelt to pray, I finally released my emotions. Until then, I had suppressed my tears, believing that showing emotion was a sign of weakness. I thought if I did, I was being selfish. I needed to remain strong and composed. However, as I began crying uncontrollably, I realized that only a miracle could save Riley. I prayed fervently for that miracle, feeling a sense of relief wash over me. I discovered a newfound strength and resolve in that moment, knowing we would weather this storm regardless of the outcome. We had the power of God's will supporting us. We drew resilience from our faith and the constant assistance of our incredible medical team. Throughout those dreadful days, Pat Furlong stood by our side, offering encouragement and serving as the pillar of our support system. She never left our side.

This Wait is Over!

You wait your whole life for a moment, and then one day, it's here. It was a Friday afternoon when the most glorious sound we had ever heard started beeping in our pockets. It was the sound we had been eagerly anticipating all our lives. That sound signified that a heart was available for Riley. Our pagers had been activated in the hospital.

Our medical team swiftly joined us to prep Riley for the transplant. While we were aware that we had a long road ahead of us, our shared excitement was palpable. The anticipation for Riley's procedure was not limited to us; everyone around us was equally thrilled for him.

Karen Uzark, Riley's heart transplant coordinator, arrived promptly and assured us of her continuous support from the very beginning to the conclusion of the transplant. She conveyed that despite the availability of a heart for transplant, we weren't out of the woods yet.

The donor heart was being sourced from another hospital and would then be transported to *Cincinnati Children's Hospital* for Riley's operation. In a scene reminiscent of a movie, the heart would be transported in a small red Playmate cooler. Upon its arrival, the transplant doctor and his team would meticulously examine the heart. No matter how minor, any imperfection (even as minuscule as a slight bruise) would disqualify it from being transplanted into Riley. Therefore, Riley had to be prepared for the procedure as if it were happening imminently. Time was of the essence, and everyone involved needed to be fully prepared for what was yet to come.

The wait proved to be the hardest part. Finally, at around 6:30 p.m., we got the thumbs up! We received the long-awaited confirmation: Riley was set to receive his new heart. As the medical team prepared Riley for the procedure, they instructed him to remove his necklace. This request, however, unsettled him, and he expressed his reluctance to proceed with the surgery unless he could keep the necklace close. After a brainstorming session, a solution was found: the medical team securely fastened the necklace around Riley's ankle using tape to ensure it stayed in place during the procedure. With his LUCKY charm beside him, nothing was stopping him now.

We hugged, kissed, and said our goodbyes. The next time we see Riley, he will be a new kid with a new heart.

There is a poem called *Footprints* by Margaret Fishback Powers, and the last sentence says,

> He whispered,
>
> "My precious child, I love you and will never leave you.
>
> Never, ever, during your trials and testings.
>
> When you saw only one set of footprints,
>
> It was then that I carried you."[22]

Right then, I knew God was carrying all three of us.

Ron and I were escorted into the waiting room as the transplant procedure got underway. We were informed that it would span four to six hours. Karen, Riley's transplant coordinator, assured us that she would intermittently update us on Riley's progress. We found ourselves with only each other and our thoughts. It seemed that was all we needed and all we would ever need. Ron and I had experienced so much with Riley. He had been with us throughout our entire marriage. We had never known a life without him and didn't want to start now.

As the hours ticked by - one, two, three, four, five --Karen kept her promise and briefed us on Riley's condition. To our relief, he was faring well. She shared with us the joy she experienced in witnessing a new heartbeat for the first time, emphasizing that it was a moment that never lost its magic. When Ron inquired if Riley's new heart would require a shock to start beating, Karen explained that once connected and filled with blood, the heart would naturally begin its rhythm and start beating on its own.

Finally, the transplant was successfully completed at 1:30 a.m. on March 31, 2007. Riley was the proud new owner of a heart picked out especially for him. Overwhelmed with happiness, Ron and I embraced each other, tears of gratitude streaming down our faces. The efforts of *Cincinnati*

Children's Hospital, *Parent Project Muscular Dystrophy*, and Pat Furlong had unequivocally saved Riley's life.

Following the transplant, the surgeon approached us to discuss the procedure. He vividly described how Riley's old heart had been severely enlarged. It was indeed a miracle he was still alive. The surgeon reassured us that Riley had responded exceptionally well to the surgery, and the transplant had been a triumph. He elaborated on the slightly prolonged duration of the operation, attributing it to the need for additional titanium to sew up Riley's rib cage. Due to his *DMD*, his weakened rib cage was like mush once they opened him up.

We experienced five fleeting minutes of unbelievable happiness, and then BAM! Reality hit us hard. "The Beast's" unrelenting attack on the rest of Riley's body was at it again. Fortunately, his new heart was free from *DMD* and would never degenerate because of it. This time, we were determined not to let it defeat us. We could not have hoped for a better outcome.

Riley, who had defied all expectations, became one of the earliest ambulatory heart transplant recipients with *DMD* in the WORLD.

We had the right doctors, hospital, community of angels, and our most extraordinary gift, Pat Furlong.

Be realistic about a heart transplant. Plan for a Miracle!

We planned for a miracle, and it happened!

"Use your knowledge and your heart to stand up for those who can't stand, speak for those who can't speak, be a beacon of light for those whose lives have become dark." Quote by Julie Andrews

Pat was our beacon of light!

We were placed on this earth to assist Riley on his journey through life. God selected us to be Riley's parents because He knew we were up to the task.

When Riley was ten, we were informed that if he ever required a transplant, it was unlikely that his body would survive the procedure. HE PROVED THEM ALL WRONG!

There is HOPE! There is always HOPE!

Chapter 6: Aftermath

There is always personal triumph over tragedy. In Riley's case, tragedy meant that someone had to lose their life so he could continue with his. After the transplant, if you listened closely enough, you could almost hear a collective sigh of relief from everyone who had been praying, with hope and faith, that Riley would pull through and receive his new heart. We put all our eggs in one basket, and this strategy paid off.

It was reminiscent of "Hands Across America," with support coming from *CCH*, *PPMD*, and the local Helena community during the fundraiser event. Riley is an example of thinking the unthinkable can be done; it was done, and the outcome was tremendous, awe-inspiring, and beautiful.

Prayers Answered

When you face death on a daily basis, fear gradually fades away. You learn to accept it, to ready yourself for its arrival, never knowing when it might come. The waiting period for the completion of the transplant felt like an eternity as we sat in anticipation. The uncertainty between updates was the most challenging part. Each time we received new information, I hurried to call my family. Greg, Dave, and Maria had gathered at our home to provide support to Lexi, my mom, and my dad. I was immensely grateful for their unwavering presence. Upon the completion of the transplant, my first call was to Lexi. As I shared the incredible news over the phone, everyone present at our home rejoiced. The overwhelming sense of relief and gratitude filled the room as we realized our prayers had been answered. Riley will have a new heart!

The sound of my mom's joy brought a profound sense of peace. Despite the hardships she had endured, especially following my dad's hip injury, she remained stoic and resilient. In the background, Dave's voice could be heard exclaiming, "It's about time!" You could hear everyone in the background whooping and hollering. "Finally, something good has happened for Riley," Dave concluded. I would have to agree wholeheartedly.

The rest of the family members and friends received phone calls with the same astonishing news. They were in disbelief, yet deep down, they knew that a miracle had taken place.

In the face of our family's challenges, my parents always emphasized the importance of finding the silver lining. As the saying goes, every cloud has a silver lining. We had prepared for the worst while hoping and praying for the best. This was our moment, our silver lining!

Three Magical Words

I remember Ron and me reassuring Riley that everything would be okay just before they wheeled him out of the room for his surgery, knowing that he would soon have a new heart and a fresh perspective on life. We had to stay strong for him, but honestly, we didn't know if we would ever see our son again during that moment.

The difference was already visible when we saw him after the operation -- his cheeks had regained color, and he appeared more vibrant and alive than we had seen him in years. In the *ICU*, Ron and I held his hands as he regained consciousness, and with tears in his eyes, he looked up at us and said, "I CAN BREATHE!"

Those were the three most magical words we had ever heard. While we knew that the next few days would be critical for Riley's recovery, at that moment, we felt like the luckiest parents in the world.

Walking around, it felt as though we had just won the lottery; Riley got his much-deserved transplant. We were very grateful but also very humbled by it all. We knew that someone else had to die for Riley to live. We also learned that it took an extraordinary person to become a donor in the first place. Doing so and knowing that you can potentially save numerous people's lives is truly an act of love. We were honored to know that someone else's selfless act saved Riley's life.

In the midst of it all, Pat Furlong stood out as our guardian angel. She was the constant we needed, and her tireless efforts to save Riley's life were nothing short of miraculous. I am Catholic, and she is as close to "sainthood" as one can be. We will forever be indebted to her and grateful for her role in Riley's journey.

The first night Riley spent in the *ICU*, we watched his chest intently. Every time he inhaled and exhaled, it felt like a gift from God. His lung capacity was already showing significant improvement, and his heart and lungs grew stronger with each breath.

Over the next few days in the *ICU*, we never left Riley's side, watching over him as he was surrounded by a maze of tubes and wires, resembling something out of a sci-fi movie. We affectionately referred to the array of machines as the "mothership panel." The medical team closely monitored him to ensure the success of the transplant and his body's acceptance of the new heart.

On the third day, Pat was right by our side as we prepared to transport Riley to another lab for a cardiac MRI. This was a critical test to assess how his new heart was functioning. The task of moving him required a coordinated effort, with everyone pitching in. Not only did we have to move him, but we also had to transport the mothership panel, adding to the complexity of the task. We managed to manipulate all the necessary equipment with patience and careful handling. Ron, Pat, and I were enlisted to help. Together, we formed a somewhat mismatched team as we navigated the hallways of the vast hospital to reach the MRI room. Fortunately, the MRI results were positive, signaling that Riley's new heart was adapting well.

Witnessing the marvel of modern science and technology as Riley's body embraced another's heart still amazes us to this day. We have been so blessed to be a part of this miracle that has given Riley a second chance at life.

Last Rites

Cincinnati Children's Hospital was renowned for its treatment of boys with *DMD*, and time and time again, *CCH* and *PPMD* collaborated to provide comprehensive care. Every night, I thank my lucky stars because they were the lifeline we needed to help Riley through his horrific ordeal.

Ron and I were fortunate to have met some astounding people through *PPMD*. We built a strong network of parents whose sons were affected by this terrible disease. Soon after Riley's transplant, one of the families was traveling from Florida to *CCH* with their son for spinal fusion surgery. Ron stayed in touch with Kevin and Jackie Smith, Zach's parents, and knew they would be arriving in the next few days. *PPMD* had arranged for them to stay in the same Condo complex where we lived, and we wanted to make their stay extra special to ensure they didn't feel alone during this challenging time.

Ron obtained an extra key to their Condo and went to the grocery store to surprise them with essential items before their arrival. I told Ron it was okay to go because there was no way I would leave Riley. He promised to return quickly and hurried off to run the errand.

Alone in the room with Riley, I held his hand, reflecting on the arduous journey that had led me to this moment. The task of reaching this point had been monumental, yet here he lay before me, his chest rising and falling with each breath. It was like he was reborn. With his new heart, free from *DMD*, it was truly a priceless gift. The assurance that this heart within him was immune to the constant threat of "The Beast" brought me utter jubilation. Even now, seventeen years later, reminiscing about that moment still makes me smile.

I cherished basking in the glow of this new revelation and having this private moment with Riley. Staring at his cherubic face, I noticed something amiss. His face began to tremble, followed by his entire body. Alarms from the machines sounded, and I saw foam coming from his mouth.

The following moments were chaotic; nurses and doctors rushed in, pushing me aside. Riley was experiencing a seizure, and it looked serious. Amid the frenzy, a nurse inquired about Ron's whereabouts and explained that I needed to contact him ASAP. When I got word to him, he immediately dropped everything and rushed back to the hospital

In the meantime, I was left alone with just my thoughts. What was going on? How could it go from being so magical to being so life-threatening? Are we going to lose Riley?

Shortly after, a priest arrived to comfort me. As he held my hand, we prayed together. Our steadfast Catholic faith has consistently helped us navigate difficult situations. I knew that relying on that faith and hope would be essential for me at this moment.

As the situation grew bleak, he sought approval to offer prayers and administer the Last Rites to Riley. How could this turn of events be unfolding? Amidst the chaotic scene, he started his prayer for Riley, and tears welled up in my eyes. The urge to collapse and surrender overwhelmed me. Yet, at that moment, the priest's words filled my ears, drowning out everything else. I found myself silently reciting the Lord's Prayer and Hail Mary. These familiar prayers naturally come to mind in moments of distress, offering me solace and peace.

And just like that! As soon as it began, it ended! Riley had clawed his way back, displaying a remarkable will to live. By the time Ron returned, the storm had passed, and calmness prevailed. All was right with the world once again.

However, "The Beast" was back! Due to the severity of the seizure, Riley was prescribed a medication called Keppra. This marked the start of a long list of medications Riley would need to take. Adding this new medication to the regimen was another source of concern. Fortunately, Riley only had to take it for a brief period. It seemed that this was an isolated incident. Whew!

ICU Psychosis[23]

ICU Psychosis, also called intensive care unit syndrome, is when people develop serious psychiatric symptoms of delirium unique to the ICU environment. There are often emotional or personality changes with frequent mood changes such as anger, agitation, anxiety, apathy, depression, fear, euphoria, irritability, or suspicion. You may have changes in sleep patterns, memory loss, disorganized thinking, or just going through the motions.

Ron and I began exhibiting signs of ICU Psychosis when Riley was initially admitted to the hospital. Unbeknownst to us, Linda Cripe and Kathy Kinnet had been closely monitoring our behavior. They observed that I was struggling more than Ron. I started refusing to leave the hospital and even avoided going to the cafeteria to grab a meal, fearing that I might miss something crucial if I stepped away. I was left alone when Riley experienced cardiac arrest and a seizure shortly after the transplant. This situation further heightened my anxiety and unease.

Until that moment, my entire life revolved around caring for others. I can still vividly recall the day when Linda Cripe and Kathy Kinnet entered Riley's room and informed me that they were taking me to the cafeteria for lunch. I hesitated at first, only agreeing because Ron was on duty. They shared with me some profound words of wisdom to uplift my spirits. "Consider the hospital your temporary residence, so set out the welcome mat because you'll have plenty of (visitors). Pick yourself up, brush off the dust, and carry on. It's essential to maintain a sense of normalcy. Shower daily, put on some makeup, enjoy a proper meal, and treat the hospital as your home. Take pride in yourself, not just for your sake, but for your son's."

"Regardless of how challenging things may seem, strive to approach each day as if you were at home. During a prolonged hospital stay, it's easy to neglect self-care. Remember, you must prioritize your well-being because only then can you provide the best care for Riley. Your son will truly need you once he leaves this hospital. That's when the real journey begins. Don't lose sight of who you are, how you arrived here, and where you're headed." Their advice was empowering.

Those invaluable words of wisdom have remained with me throughout the years. These remarkable women took the time to ensure I reached my full potential. Despite their busy schedules, they made a point to pull me aside and offer guidance during this tumultuous period. Although it initially seemed far-fetched, they could see the path Ron and I were heading down. I had to stop feeling sorry for myself because Riley needed us to be his parents. It was the most encouraging pep talk I ever received. I took their advice to heart, started to take showers, dress up, and apply makeup. These simple actions made a world of difference, helping me regain a sense of normalcy and feel like myself again.

Since *CCH* was a teaching hospital, we had many visitors. As the number of visitors started to become overwhelming, we realized the need to establish some boundaries. Kathy Kinnet and Linda Cripe continued to offer me words of encouragement whenever they noticed me feeling down. We began to treat Riley's hospital room as our own sanctuary. The room had three regular walls and one large glass wall for doctors and nurses to monitor him. At times, it felt like we were living in a fishbowl. To ensure moments of peace and rest, we would draw the curtains and hang a sign on the window indicating that we were resting and preferred not to be disturbed unless it was an emergency. We learned to expect privacy, and in return, it was respected.

Ron and I decided to take turns staying with Riley at night. One of us would stay in the room with him, while the other would rest in a sleeping room provided by the hospital. These small and windowless sleeping rooms created a dark and quiet environment for much-needed rest. After about two weeks, we said goodbye to the sleeping rooms. One of us would stay with him in the ICU and the other would go back to our little Condo unit for some rest and relaxation.

To maintain our sanity during this challenging time, we devised a game to cope with the disruptions of the night. We kept a tally on a whiteboard of the various disturbances that woke us up in the hospital ICU, such as beeping machines, bathroom trips for Riley, blood draws by nurses or any other interruptions. In our little competition, Ron emerged as the winner with 38 disturbances compared to my 35 in a single night. They were long nights indeed. You don't get much rest in a hospital ICU.

The nursing staff at *CCH* was incredible. They were compassionate and devoted individuals who clearly had a deep passion for their work. We affectionately referred to them as our angels. Overall, our experiences with the nursing staff were good. There were, however, a few incidents that were more memorable than others.

One memorable day, Riley managed to persuade one of the nurses to remove the catheter he had been fitted with since his surgery. However, later that evening, during the doctors' rounds, they instructed the nurse to reinsert it. As everyone gathered around his bed, the nurse bravely carried out the procedure despite Riley's excruciating pain, prompting him to exclaim, "Whoever came up with this procedure is a FRICKING idiot." Initially taken aback by his outburst, the doctors couldn't help but burst into laughter as they realized the truth in his words.

On a separate occasion, when Ron was staying with Riley, they were both fast asleep when a nurse on her rounds approached Riley, shook his shoulders, and asked if he was awake. Ron, who overheard, responded loudly, "He is now!" Needless to say, she never disturbed his sleep again.

During another visit, I was by Riley's side when a nurse came in to tend to him. She noticed remnants of medical tape from his surgery still stuck on after his transplant. Gently removing the tape, she uncovered scars on his stomach that had formed the shape of a smiley face. This unique mark stayed with him for years, serving as a quirky reminder of his transplant journey before eventually fading away.

Ten Second Ted

When you spend considerable time in the hospital, you should never forget your sense of humor. The saying "laughter is the best medicine" is believed to have originated — albeit now in a snappier form —from Proverbs 17.22 of the *King James Bible*. But it's more than a proverb. Both medical and spiritual experts have long recognized the power of laughter.

After relocating to Cincinnati, Ohio, for the transplant procedure, we embraced the city's sports teams as our own. From supporting the Cincinnati Bengals in professional football to rooting for Ohio State in football and basketball, we also enjoyed cheering on the Cincinnati Reds in baseball. The warm reception we received from the people of Cincinnati made us feel right at home, and we quickly realized that Ohioans, aside from Montanans, are some of the most welcoming individuals.

As previously mentioned in earlier chapters, Riley is an avid sports enthusiast, particularly during the month of March when he immerses himself in the excitement of college basketball's March Madness. Throughout the tournament, you'll find him at home, diligently watching each and every game. How does he manage to do this, you may wonder? It's all thanks to our investment in satellite TV and DVR technology. Riley has perfected the skill of recording every game, allowing him to relish watching them at his own pace.

The March Madness Tournament that particular year commenced on March 13, 2007, and concluded on April 2, 2007. Florida clinched the *NCAA* title once again by triumphing over Ohio State in the championship game with a score of 84–75.

During Riley's hospital stay, he made sure to catch as many March Madness games as possible, eagerly following the journey of the 64 teams down to The Final Four. It so happened that The Final Four games coincided with Riley's transplant day on March 31. Looking ahead, the Championship game was scheduled for April 2, 2007, a date Riley had marked on his calendar with hopeful anticipation for an Ohio State victory. Riley's emotions ran high when it came to his favorite teams, and the highs and lows of their performance deeply affected him.

As the Championship game unfolded, Riley, still recovering from the transplant, found himself drifting in and out of consciousness. His mind was a whirlwind of thoughts, at times coherent and, at others, nonsensical. Despite his condition, there were moments of humor amidst the seriousness as Riley uttered amusing and outlandish remarks, prompting laughter among those around him.

Occasionally, he would lucidly inquire about the game's outcome, rooting for his team, Ohio State. Unfortunately, Ohio State lost, and we were hesitant to deliver the disheartening news to him. However, Riley persisted, demanding to know the score. Upon learning of his team's defeat, he would dramatically throw his arms up in the air and let out a resounding "UGH!" We found ourselves in fits of laughter, only for him to soon slip back into unconsciousness. This scenario would repeat every 10 to 20 minutes throughout the day. We would feel anxious about informing him because it would trigger another round of the same behavior. Subsequently, he would become upset because we couldn't contain our laughter.

Dr. Spicer walked in on that day as Riley was waking up. Curiously, Riley inquired about the game's outcome, and upon hearing Dr. Spicer's response, his theatrics kicked in once more! The doctor found this reaction quite amusing, leading us to nickname Riley "Ten Second Ted" affectionately due to his occasional short-term memory lapses.

Once, when he was out of it, he started acting like a WWII soldier. He started making gun sounds and telling us he was killing Nazis. Another time, he told us he was eating popcorn with Dan Marino on the moon. Dan Marino was his favorite quarterback, and he used to play for the Miami Dolphins, his favorite football team.

In one incident, Riley gave the anesthesiologist a specific order from Subway when he started to doze off. The doctor remembered his order and went to Subway to get him a sandwich. When he came out of sedation, a foot-long sub, exactly as he had ordered, was waiting for him in his room. So, Riley making off-beat statements was par for the course, and the staff at *CCH* loved him for it!

Momento to Last a Lifetime

Riley's transplant was so miraculous that I wanted to remember every detail, feeling it was essential never to forget. A week before the transplant, on March 22, I celebrated my 38th birthday. To mark this special occasion, Ron surprised me with a sterling silver necklace adorned with two hearts and a matching heart bracelet. The two hearts on the necklace symbolize Riley and Lexi, making it a truly poignant moment in our lives. His thoughtfulness in remembering my birthday made it even more special.

On the day of the transplant, I put on the necklace and bracelet. I distinctly remember wearing a light blue V-neck sweater over a white t-shirt paired with dark blue velour sweatpants. Although I no longer wear those clothes, I have kept them stashed away along with the jewelry. To this day, I still wear the jewelry, cherishing the memories it holds.

Spring Break

The last time we saw Lexi, she had two casts, one on each wrist, and tears streamed down her face as she waved to me from the airport gate. We missed her dearly and eagerly anticipated her arrival. She was coming to spend her Spring Break with us. Meanwhile, Riley remained in the ICU, appearing disheveled and exhausted. I don't believe she was ready for what awaited her.

Ron picked her up from the airport and drove her straight to the hospital. When I saw her, I couldn't believe my eyes. She had transformed from the frightened little girl I remembered at the airport into a blossoming teenager. She would be turning 13 in June, starting to show her age. During our time apart, she had her casts removed and braces placed on her teeth. While I regretted missing these important milestones in her life, I was grateful she could experience them with my mom and dad.

When she entered the room and laid eyes on Riley, she gasped and instinctively covered her mouth. Tears welled up in her eyes, clearly showing how deeply shocked she was by what she saw. Riley had recently undergone a life-saving heart transplant, and his road to recovery would be a taxing one. It would take a while to get him back into fighting shape. As soon as he caught sight of her, a radiant smile illuminated his face, brightening the entire room. He was overjoyed to be reunited with her once again.

Riley was administered a high dose of Morphine to alleviate the pain, causing his stomach to bloat and giving him a severely emaciated appearance. This physical change initially frightened Lexi. Riley's weight had plummeted to a mere 75 lbs. When we helped him stand, his distended belly felt as taut as a basketball.

It was then that she truly grasped the extent of Riley's illness. When you're near someone every day, it's easy to overlook the gradual changes or subtleties in their appearance. The realization of how unwell Riley was left her heartbroken. Her compassion and empathy towards her older brother were truly admirable.

Lexi provided us with a much-needed boost during the entire week she stayed with us. She was the perfect distraction. Given Riley's limited mobility, we spent our time watching TV (mostly sports), playing games, and discussing all the activities Riley could look forward to with his new heart.

As a family, we discussed planning a special trip to celebrate Riley's ability to travel again. We asked him to choose our destination, and Riley expressed his desire to revisit Maui. We had previously visited the island as a Christmas gift for my parents when Riley was seven and Lexi was five.

Nina, Ron, Riley, Lexi

A plan was devised for Riley to be discharged from the hospital, return to Montana, and begin his freshman year of high school. Once the doctors cleared us for more travel, we would head back to Maui. Everything seemed to be falling into place perfectly.

By the time Lexi's Spring Break came to an end, Riley had made remarkable progress. The pallor of his skin had vanished, and his energy levels had surged significantly. With his new heart in place, he found it easier to breathe, and his endurance showed a marked improvement. His body had grown accustomed to his old heart, so taking a deep breath now felt like a luxury. He was being nourished with 3,000-calorie milkshakes between meals, and we could see some healthy weight gain on his previously slender frame. Following Lexi's return home, Riley was transferred to a different floor housing the regular rooms, signaling the beginning of the next phase of his recovery journey. Here, the real work was poised to commence.

Birthday Boy

Eleven days after undergoing his life-saving transplant, Riley celebrated his 15th birthday on April 11, 2007. At this point, his recovery was progressing smoothly. He had already begun to stand up and walk independently. Witnessing him walk the length of the hallway left us STUNNED! We were astonished by his remarkable progress. It was incredible to see how quickly he regained his strength and vitality. *DMD* didn't ravage the new heart, and a rejuvenated Riley emerged.

Despite our limited surroundings, I wanted to do something special to celebrate this incredible milestone in his life. After speaking with the hospital staff, we decided to organize a small celebration in the teen room on Riley's floor. I went to the store and purchased a cake and decorations to liven up the space. Wanting to surprise Riley, I felt a spontaneous gesture would bring much-needed excitement into his life. We suggested that it would be beneficial to get some exercise, so we accompanied him to the teen room. As he entered, he was greeted by everyone who had been a part of his odyssey to 15 years old. The overwhelming show of support truly surprised him on this momentous day. The presence of Pat and Linda was essential to making it a true celebration. Witnessing Riley's progress, everyone present rejoiced in his well-being. It was a testament to how a little effort can make a significant impact. Riley had achieved the impossible! Here's to 15 years and beyond…

Recovery

When faced with a condition as serious as *DMD*, your life is a series of baby steps. Riley still had a long way to go, but progress was being made, one small step at a time. He was eager to return to our apartment in Cincinnati, yearning for a semblance of normalcy in our lives. Ensuring he received all his heart-rejection medications on schedule was something we were going to have to master. With nearly 40 pills to take each day, the timing was everything – doses were set for 8 am, 4 pm, and 8 pm, and it was imperative not to overlap them. In addition to the medication regimen, Riley had numerous appointments and blood draws to monitor his levels closely. Before being discharged, the medical team needed to be confident that we, as parents, were equipped to manage this responsibility effectively. Fully committed, we embraced the challenge wholeheartedly. The doctors emphasized to Riley the critical importance of adhering to this strict routine, as his life hinged on it. A heart transplant is a life-altering event that demands unwavering dedication and readiness for the long road ahead.

A few days before Riley was discharged, I decided to grab a cup of coffee in the common area. While there, I struck up a conversation with a mother who was also present. She shared with me that her son had undergone a heart transplant a few years back. In turn, I mentioned Riley's recent surgery and our anticipation of returning home soon.

The mother appeared haggard and visibly distressed as she recounted her challenges. This was the second time her son had been hospitalized due to non-compliance with his heart medication. Regrettably, during his first admission, he had lost sight in one eye as a consequence. The current situation was equally dreadful, and she was uncertain about the potential complications her son might encounter.

She confided in me about the difficulties of being a single parent and the struggles she encountered in persuading her 17-year-old son to adhere to his medication regimen. Believing himself to be impervious to harm, he would often stop taking his medication once he felt better, considering it too cumbersome. Monitoring him and enforcing a strict schedule proved to be an ongoing battle for her. Her poignant narrative left me deeply moved and saddened by the circumstances she and her son were facing.

After experiencing everything alongside Riley and Ron, there was no way I was going to let that happen to him. I wished her luck and silently thanked God and my lucky stars that I wasn't in her shoes. The fate of that young man remained a mystery to me as I never crossed paths with her again. Upon returning to the room, I relayed the disturbing story to Riley and Ron, and they were equally shocked. Riley, reflecting on his own brush with death, confidently declared, "That will never be me. I've been given a second chance at life, and I won't waste it." Words spoken like a true survivor.

A month after Riley was admitted to *CCH*, he walked out of the hospital of his own volition, empowered by his new heart. He was ready to take on the world.

The Boy Who Lived

The day Riley was discharged from the hospital was truly a momentous occasion. Although we still needed to remain in Cincinnati for his routine checkups and careful monitoring, the prospect of living life beyond the hospital walls filled us with gratitude. Riley demonstrated a

138

strong commitment to his studies, and during his time in the hospital, I had the privilege of continuing to tutor him. With much thanks and gratitude to C.R. Anderson Middle School back in Montana, Riley was able to complete 8th grade along with his fellow students. He was looking forward to starting his freshman year at Capital High School in Helena, Montana. We only needed to prove to Riley's team of doctors that we could do this from the comfort of home.

Besides being an excellent student, Riley always had a voracious appetite for reading. Living in Cincinnati afforded us the opportunity to explore numerous secondhand bookstores. We embarked on occasional field trips to break the monotony of our apartment life. Given Riley's deep passion for reading and my own love for sharing books with him, this activity soon evolved into a cherished weekly tradition. While Ron and Riley found common ground in sports, reading served as a special bond between Riley and I as mother and son.

Every time we visited the used bookstore, Riley would buy books ranging from 50 to 300 pages and eagerly consume them once he returned home. His insatiable reading habit led him to finish multiple books in a single day. He had a remarkable talent for speed reading and an uncanny ability to remember what he read. I struggled to keep pace with his reading speed. For Riley, immersing himself in books was a means of escaping from his troubles before and after the transplant.

Riley and I especially enjoyed reading the Harry Potter series. We were prepared when the seventh book in the series was released on July 21, 2007. We reread the first six books and eagerly anticipated purchasing the final book.

When I was able to purchase the book *Harry Potter and the Deathly Hallows*, Riley devoured the book in a day, all 784 pages. Next, it was my turn. I finished it just as quickly. We must have talked about the book for a whole week because Ron kept asking if we could change the subject. Bonding over our shared love for Harry Potter was a special time for me. It meant that, even for a moment, we could forget about all our troubles and be transported to a magical place and time. I still watch the movies and have reread the books countless times.

This book evoked nostalgic memories of a tumultuous period in our lives, allowing us a brief respite from it. The book profoundly affected both of us because it is about survival, facing death, and embracing it like an old friend instead of running away from it. You are no longer afraid because you know you tried your best, and you let the chips fall where they may. You never gave up without a fight; the hero ultimately takes all the spoils. With his remarkable courage and strength, Riley is the boy who lived!! Just like Harry Potter.

We were keeping our fingers crossed that they would allow us to return home in August. While we anxiously awaited news, we had the opportunity to discover the charms of Cincinnati and savor all it had in store. As Riley was required to wear a mask indoors, we often opted for leisurely drives, exploring various parks for delightful picnics. Cincinnati boasts a stunning cityscape, with its parks mirroring this beauty. We remained vigilant about germs during the initial 4-6 weeks following the transplant. Ron and I were the only individuals permitted to be near Riley without masks. As his primary caregivers, we understood the need for controlled germ exposure to bolster his immune system.

Donor Characteristics

Reports have appeared in medical and lay literature that after receiving a new organ, some recipients may experience traits present in their donor.[24] I believe this statement to be true. Several weeks after the transplant, it became evident Riley's palette had changed. Historically, he was not one to indulge in sweets, but he had developed an unexpected penchant for gum and hard candy. Constantly needing something to chew on or suck on, he made it a habit to request stops at the store during our daily drives to purchase these treats. While initially somewhat of an obsession, we found it endearing and happily catered to his new cravings, often sharing a laugh about it. However, after several months, this newfound fondness gradually subsided.

Making a Lasting Memory

Ron knew that Riley missed attending sporting events since the transplant, and he wanted to do something special for him. Ron had been discussing this with his friend Steve Sobonya, who was the strength coach for Fresno State at the time, and he also trained professional athletes. Steve had connections with the Cincinnati Bengals, particularly with Coach Kevin Coyle. After explaining Riley's story to Coach Coyle, a stand-up person, he immediately offered his help and invited Riley to attend a Bengals practice. Both Riley and Ron were overjoyed and eagerly accepted the once-in-a-lifetime opportunity. This outing was featured in the March 9-15, 2008, edition of the American Profile.

Coach Kevin Doyle and the Cincinnati Bengals[25]

Coach Kevin Coyle, A heart for kindness[26]

"In February 2007, 14-year-old Riley Herrera's family temporarily relocated from Helena, Mont. (pop. 25,780), to a tiny apartment in Cincinnati as Riley awaited a donor heart at *Cincinnati Children's Hospital*. Riley, who suffered from cardiomyopathy, a heart muscle disease, underwent transplant surgery a month later and spent months in Cincinnati recovering."

"'It was really boring,' recalls Riley, now 15. 'I didn't have any friends there.'"That changed one day in June when Riley got a call from the Cincinnati Bengals secondary coach, Kevin Coyle, who had heard about the teenager through a mutual friend. Coyle invited Riley to visit the football team's practice."

"'It was really neat,' Riley says. 'We got to meet all the players and we got to meet the coach and we got to do practice with them.' Riley smiled that day for the first time in months, says his father, Ron, 41. 'Riley's new heart gave him life,' Ron adds, 'but coach Coyle gave him his spirit back.'"

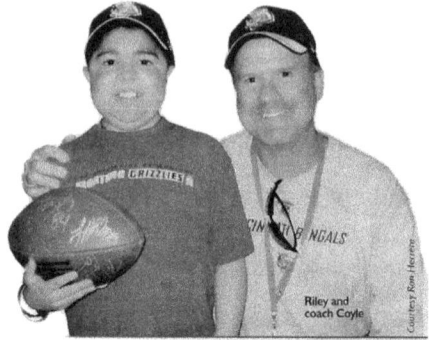

Riley, Coach Kevin Coyle

"It does make you feel good that you can brighten someone's day up just by spending some time and acknowledging them and just showing that you care," says Coyle, 52, who keeps a photo of Riley on his office wall. "Whenever any of us can take advantage of that, it's the proper thing to do. I think everybody wins."[27]

Riley and Ron joined the team for practice, and as it concluded, the players gathered around Riley while Coach Coyle delivered an inspiring

speech on perseverance. In a touching gesture, they presented Riley with a football signed by the entire team and the owner. That entire organization was the epitome of class from top to bottom.

They embarked on a tour of the team's facilities following the practice. As they passed the weight room, player TJ Houshmandzadeh motioned for Riley to join him. The two engaged in a heartfelt conversation, after which TJ removed his cleats, signed them with a Sharpie marker, and handed them to Riley. With a wave goodbye, TJ headed barefoot into the locker room, leaving Riley in awe of the whole experience. It was a surreal moment for Riley, being in the presence of professional athletes in such an intimate setting.

Riley was starting to feel homesick, and this incredible experience was just what the doctor ordered. As a result, we decided to adopt the Cincinnati Bengals as our family football team. To this day, we still find joy in watching them play. Riley even had the opportunity to attend a Cincinnati Bengals football game when he visited for one of his checkups. Once again, Coach Coyle generously blessed Riley and Ron with tickets, and they had a fantastic time.

Summer Time

We were fortunate to have Lexi stay with us during her summer break. We knew that coming together as a family was the most important thing we could do to support Riley's recovery. With the warm weather, we took advantage of our condo complex outdoor swimming pool. Swimming provided great exercise, which was critical for building up Riley's lung function after his prolonged illness and hospital stay. The kids enjoyed the convenience of being able to swim whenever they wanted, and although they missed our boating adventures back in Montana, the pool was a wonderful alternative. Riley's strength was improving week by week, and his recovery pace even surprised us.

Riley's favorite time of the year has always been the Fourth of July. We typically hosted family and friends for a barbecue, and Ron and Riley would organize a spectacular fireworks show. As the holiday approached, we pondered how to keep the kids entertained. We decided to venture to Norris Lake, Tennessee when Riley was cleared for travel. Ron diligently searched for a cozy cabin nestled in the woods and a boat rental spot. We understood how much they missed spending time at the lake and boating.

When we informed Riley and Lexi about the trip, they were overjoyed. It felt like a throwback to the good old days. Riley had returned to his former self, but even better! Sometimes, you take things for granted, and we didn't realize how his heart affected his whole body because of *DMD*. The excitement of being able to experience this first trip with him was overwhelming. The trip turned out to be exactly what we all needed.

143

We went boating and swimming and explored as much of the lake as we could. On the Fourth of July, we sat outside our cabin in the evening and enjoyed a magnificent fireworks display. It was a flawless conclusion to a wonderful excursion.

As July ended, we knew school would resume for Riley and Lexi at the end of August.

Do We Stay or Do We Go

Ron and I considered the idea of permanently moving to Cincinnati that summer. Riley had received exceptional medical care there, making the thought of returning to Montana daunting as we would be without the support we had grown accustomed to. Our heart transplant team, our *PPMD* family, Pat Furlong, and Linda Cripe were all based in Cincinnati, and the care available for *DMD* boys at *CCH* was unparalleled. With such a strong support system in place, why would we want to be anywhere else? Cincinnati had embraced us and made us feel like a part of their community.

We found ourselves at a crossroads, facing a decision that required careful consideration of the advantages and disadvantages, as it would entail a significant commitment from each of us. Should we decide to relocate, Ron would need to request a transfer within his role in the federal government, while I would be faced with the difficult choice of either selling or closing down my beloved preschool. Ron held a secure and fulfilling position, and as for me, teaching was not just a job but a true vocation that I adored. The bond I shared with my dedicated staff, the supportive parents, and the children I had the privilege of teaching made it a deeply rewarding experience.

My preschool had recently organized a major fundraiser for Riley, and Ron's colleagues generously donated their vacation time so Ron could be by Riley's side during the transplant and recovery. While Ron and I worked tirelessly to achieve our current positions, Riley's well-being held far greater significance for us. We had made sacrifices in the past for Riley's health, trusting that God would guide us in the right direction. Our children were still young, and we believed they would adapt well to a new living environment. After all, we simply uprooted and relocated to Cincinnati to

144

ensure that Riley could receive his new heart, so moving to another city would seem like a walk in the park by comparison.

Ron and I found ourselves in a place we never expected to be once again. We agreed to take time to digest this major decision and reconvene in a few days to discuss this life-changing choice. After careful consideration and reflection, we reached a decision.

"Faith is not believing that God can. It is knowing that God will."[28] This quote from Ben Stein summed up our choice the following day. Ron and I placed our trust and faith in God and made the decision that Montana was our home and Helena was where we belonged. Riley and Lexi had a lot of living to do, and we wanted them to share all of this with the people we loved and cared for the most. We needed to be home with our family and friends.

We had to convince Riley's heart team that we were ready.

Riley diligently followed all his heart team's instructions and successfully completed 8th grade without missing a beat. As he continued to make remarkable progress in his recovery, the conversation shifted towards the possibility of him returning home. Initially, Riley's heart team expressed some skepticism about the idea of him being discharged so quickly.

We assured them we would adhere to their instructions for Riley's post-transplant care. We committed to returning for regular checkups every few months despite the distance from Helena to Cincinnati, understanding that it might pose challenges for us. Our priority was for Riley to receive aftercare exclusively from *CCH*, and we made it clear we wouldn't consider alternative options. Additionally, Riley would attend *DMD* clinics during these visits, allowing us to address multiple needs in one trip. It was a no-brainer.

After accepting their terms, they agreed that we could return to Helena in the first week of August. The thought of resuming our everyday lives filled us with immense happiness. We understood that achieving this goal would require dedication and meticulous planning, but we were confident it was achievable. Remaining in the comfortable bubble we had created in Cincinnati was no longer an option. The time had come to go back – it was now or never.

Doing What It Takes

When discussing what Ron and I have been through, Linda Cripe said: "Let's reflect on the challenges you faced and the strength you found along the way. I think it's a unique story for many reasons. He has a challenging disease, and I think historically, people are hesitant to move forward and allow this patient to undergo cardiac transplantation because of the limited number of hearts available. Sometimes, they'll say if you have other mitigating factors or what would be known as a lethal genetic disorder, you wouldn't be eligible to have a heart transplant. Getting that accomplished and seeing how well he has done, I think, is really a gift to the community because we need to have this option available to more kids with muscular dystrophy."

Pat responded, "I agree with you, Linda. There's much more here. I think this is a wonderful story of a family who was committed to each other from day one. They fought very hard, and they certainly have had a success story. I think there's much more about systems that were not in place, opportunities that were just nonexistent, and barriers to be broken."

Pat continued, "First of all, long ago, when my sons were here, the heart wasn't considered worth the value because of the muscle disease.

Linda was on board, and Cincinnati Children's was definitely on board with the heart being important; it's a muscle, and we've got to take care of it. I think the Advocacy organization (*PPMD*) still believes that the heart contributes significantly to muscle disease. If we are giving up on these patients at any point in time, it really doesn't. If they couldn't have changed or at least put him in the category of *Becker muscular dystrophy*, if the cardiologist wasn't pushing, or if we weren't supporting the family moving to Cincinnati for about six months, it would not have happened. You have to line up all of these yes's,' or it doesn't go forward, and then, of course, there is the waiting for the heart process, and the transplant itself. It was a six-hour procedure. And while waiting on that procedure, we continually asked: Will it work? What will it do? Will there be rejection?

146

Will he be able to walk again? If that heart works better and restores some of the function he lost, then the decision is obvious."

Riley has always displayed a strong fighting spirit. He was raised with the belief that one should always make an effort to pursue their goals, and even if they don't succeed, the act of trying is a success in itself. This mindset has not only enabled him to navigate through challenges but also instilled in him a deep sense of empathy towards others. In a society often characterized by selfishness, Riley stands out for his selflessness. His example reminds us to pause and consider our priorities amidst the hustle and bustle of daily life. He often emphasizes the importance of altruism by saying, "If I can walk, don't park in the handicap spot. Give it to someone who needs it. I don't need it right now." He expresses disappointment when he sees others taking advantage of handicapped parking spaces.

Riley exudes an abundance of compassion, a trait that can be rare in today's society. Surrounded by supportive individuals who uplift him, he often says, "I want you to help me. I want to achieve it, but I don't want you doing it for me." He has always been the master of his own destiny.

Riley is the true hero in all of this. He wouldn't be here today without his love for life and his determination to live. There is always a solution to any problem with love, hope, faith, and a belief to do and achieve the impossible. Our life is a testament to this belief. He exemplifies the absolute willingness to survive and become stronger and healthier in the worst situations. With a perpetual optimism shining through his eyes, Riley bears the burdens of the world with remarkable grace and dignity. His resilience has seen him conquer obstacles that most of us can only imagine in our wildest dreams. He stands as a beacon of strength and fortitude, embodying the essence of what is admirable in being human.

Remarkably, Riley goes through life's trials without a hint of self-pity, a quality that inspires admiration and introspection in those around him. His example serves as a reminder of the kind of humanity we all aspire to embody. In a world that can often be difficult and harsh, Riley's presence reminds us of the inherent goodness and strength that resides within each of us and humanity when at its best.

Begin Anew

It was time to go home. Pat Furlong, *CCH*, and *PPMD* would await our periodic returns to Cincinnati for years to come.

"Get busy living or get busy dying."[29]

Riley had beaten death, so the only thing left for us to do now was to get busy living.

We manifested this outcome. You reap what you sow; we have consistently given our all for Riley. Triumph will always prevail over tragedy. The human spirit endures, and the drive to survive surpasses our wildest expectations. We have learned to roll with the punches. Riley remains resolute in refusing to succumb to "The Beast!" Defeat is not an option for him, and he will fight until the end. Imagine what changes we could make in the world if we all did that. Riley approaches each day with the mindset of making the most of it, waking up in his body and thinking, "Today is another opportunity to live life to the fullest, and that's a good day."

I have always been private and preferred to handle things on my own. While some may view this as secretive, I see it as being protective. I was raised in an environment where self-reliance was valued, and it was ingrained in me that my problems were mine to solve. My mother, too, kept family matters within the immediate family circle. I chose not to confide in others about our difficulties because I didn't want to impose on anyone. I simply felt unable to open up. I kept things to myself because I believed I had to manage them independently.

There's an old saying, "You can take the girl out of the city, but you can't take the city out of the girl." I've learned that you can take the girl out of Butte, but you can't take Butte out of the girl. I've learned to embrace this statement. All my values and beliefs have come from growing up in Butte. It has made me strong, persistent, and a "never take 'no' for an answer" type of person. Thanks, Mom. I couldn't have gotten through this without you. Butte tough, sprinkled with a dash of sensitivity and love. That's what little Butte girls are made of.

148

Writing this book has been very cathartic for me. I have been able to bare my feelings and share what we went through and continue to encounter to this day.

We packed all our belongings in our little Toyota Camry and said goodbye to our time in Cincinnati. Saying goodbye was bittersweet because it ended the battle we had just won. "The Beast" was at bay, and we were heading home with a whole new perspective of what it means to defy the odds. We came, we saw, and Riley kicked its butt.

Ron would drive home to Helena alone because we needed every square inch of that car to fit all of our belongings. The car looked like we had just stuffed 50 pounds into a 10-pound bag. He dropped us off at the airport, and we knew the next time we saw him, Riley would begin his new life back home in Helena, Montana, with a new heart.

We were filled with anticipation as we prepared to return home and embrace a sense of normalcy again. Our time in Cincinnati had profoundly transformed each of us, shaping us into versions of ourselves we had never imagined. The connections we forged with Pat Furlong and *Cincinnati Children's Hospital* will endure for a lifetime. Our fervent wish is to exceed their expectations by providing Riley with a life filled with love and opportunities. After all, they had just saved his life; it was the least Ron and I could do. We were going to give him **The Life of Riley.**

It was time to go home and begin again.

There is HOPE! There is always HOPE!

Dianne DeMille, Ph.D. and Nina Stuart Herrera

Chapter 7: Homecoming … and Beyond

Home Sweet Home

There is a saying, "Parting is such sweet sorrow." That's how we felt the moment the four Musketeers all left the home we knew in Ohio and returned to our familiar surroundings of Helena, MT. It was truly exhilarating to know that Riley was essentially getting a fresh start. With his new heart, he would have the strength and courage to embrace each day to the fullest.

Being home was such a relief! We were happy just to be sleeping in our own beds. Family and friends stopped by to welcome us back. My parents were overjoyed when they saw us. They had done all the heavy lifting by taking care of Lexi while she finished 7th grade. We couldn't have done it without them. They had been our rocks through this whole process. I could tell by the look in their eyes that they finally had some peace. They could return to Butte knowing we were in a good place.

Greg and Dave were delighted at the prospect of Riley being given a second chance. My sister Maria and brother Chris savored the joy everyone felt upon Riley's success. Ron's family was thrilled that we were finally home and could start living again. We felt truly blessed to have endured this traumatic experience and emerged with a sense of renewed hope and faith. If we could overcome this challenge, we believed we could overcome anything.

That first night home was special because Riley had made it through hell and back. I remember getting up in the middle of the night to check on him. It seemed like I was living in a dream. From January to March, Riley was dying. Now, he was sleeping soundly in his own bed like nothing ever happened. He was almost angelic, lying there so calm and quiet. With every breath he took, I could see his chest rise and fall. It was so rhythmic, that I found myself mesmerized by how comfortable he was sleeping. It was only a few months ago that he was lying in a hospital, coughing just to keep his heart beating. Those horrible images are still branded in my mind. Riley had come so far, and it was only a matter of how far he could go from here.

One thing I knew for sure was that this new heart beating inside of Riley would last for a long time.

From that night onward and throughout the first year following the transplant, I made it a routine to check in on Riley. I would often find myself drifting off to sleep on the couch near his bedroom, ensuring I was close by. My foremost priority was to be a constant source of support for him, and he found comfort in knowing that I was always there for him.

Every night, I would quietly approach his bedroom door, leaving it slightly ajar as I stole a glance inside to confirm his breathing. Perhaps it may seem irrational, but I was haunted by the fear of discovering him motionless. The anxiety of wanting him to be safe and sound consumed me, fueling my nightly vigil.

He is 31 years old, and even now, from time to time, I catch myself checking on him in the middle of the night for reassurance. I find solace in watching the gentle rise and fall of his chest. The impact of experiencing something as life-altering as this is something that lingers. Despite not being the one who underwent the transplant, the repercussions are everlasting. A mother's work is never done.

Bringing a child into this world can be the greatest joy of someone's life. You never want to outlive your child. I hope I never meet that fate.

Keeping it together

Being back home felt comforting, but we understood a substantial amount of work was still awaiting us. One of our main priorities was organizing our schedules to accommodate Riley's regular heart checkups in Cincinnati. Ron and I took turns accompanying Riley on these trips, ensuring he took his medication on time and completing any necessary follow-up tasks before our visits to Cincinnati.

We had to return to Cincinnati the following month for another heart checkup. These checkups were no simple matter, as they involved a meticulous heart biopsy procedure to monitor any signs of rejection. Initially, they were conducted every few days, eventually transitioning to weekly, monthly, and then to annual visits.

Riley was registered to attend his freshman year at *Capital High School.* Lexi would be entering eighth grade at *C.R. Anderson,* and Ron would be back at work for the Feds in Helena, Mt. I still had *Early Movement Preschool,* and the prospect of starting the new year the first week of September was becoming increasingly overwhelming.

My staff and parents had been wonderful during my absence. They all chipped in to fill in the gaps I had left behind. One of my parents, Jen Ahmann, took on the tremendous task of running the summer program for me in my absence. I was incredibly grateful but torn about how I was going to make sure Riley started high school on a good foot while handling a full-time business. It became glaringly obvious that I was going to have to make a tough decision about my career.

I carefully listed all the advantages and disadvantages of keeping the preschool open. After careful consideration, I came to the heart-wrenching conclusion that closing the preschool was the best decision for Riley's well-being. Putting his needs above all else, I made the difficult but selfless choice. My dedicated staff members, Calesta Jackson and Sheri Gibson, were the first individuals I informed, who had shown constant support throughout this strenuous time. They had been my pillars of strength during Riley's transplant journey, consistently putting in hard work and dedication to keep the preschool running smoothly. Their understanding and willingness to assist me in the closure process were truly invaluable.

I informed the parents of children who were enrolled for the upcoming year, allowing them time to seek out another preschool. While they were understandably disappointed, they expressed gratitude for the advanced notice, enabling them to explore alternative options.

Over the next couple of weeks, I focused on preparing the preschool for a huge garage sale. I sold all my equipment and teaching aids, allowing me to give the preschool a proper send-off. A saying resonates with me during this time: "When one door closes, another one opens." As I embarked on a new chapter post-heart transplant, so did Riley, Lexi, and Ron.

Despite being back home, returning to our old routines wasn't an option. During our first year back, Ron and I made around 12 cross-country trips to and from Cincinnati. Our frequent travels allowed us to accumulate a significant number of sky miles, and we were grateful to have the support of charitable foundations to help cover the costs of these trips.

Back to School

I had arranged a meeting with the Vice Principal at *Capital High School*, Walt Chancy, to ensure a smooth transition. It was of vital importance to keep Riley's teachers and the administration abreast of his medical needs and constant appointments. Despite his recent heart transplant, Riley was able to begin his freshman year alongside his classmates at *Capital High*. Just back in March, he was dying from heart failure, and now he would be going to high school. Riley strikes again!

Even though Riley received a life-saving heart transplant, that didn't mean that things would return to normal. We had to adjust to a new normal, with Riley now living with a new heart but still facing the challenges of dealing with *DMD*. Walt Chancy ensured that Riley had all the necessary accommodations. This included access to the elevator, permission to leave 5 minutes early to reach his next class, and the continuation of his *Individualized Education Program* (*IEP*) from middle school. This allowed Riley to receive extra assistance and time for tests and completing tasks related to his education. The principal made these arrangements seem effortless.

I knew I could contact him regarding Riley, and he would get on it as soon as possible. Come to find out, he made everyone feel that way. There was something special about how he treated his students and their parents who crossed his path. Mr. Chancy used to patrol the hall during class. One particular time, he walked by Riley's classroom and happened to peek in the window. The bell rang, and everyone started to get up to leave. Riley tried to get up from his desk, but his leg gave out, leaving him sprawled out on the floor. Mr. Chancy rushed right in and picked him up. He had the uncanny ability to be at the right place at the right time. He would be there countless times throughout Riley's high school years. I don't know how we could have done it without him.

Papa

My mom and dad had moved back to their house in Butte, MT, after Lexi came to visit us in Cincinnati for the summer. They had found comfort in knowing we were all together again as a family and that Riley was going to be fine.

Although not typically affectionate, my dad held a special place in his heart for Riley and Lexi. They affectionately called him Papa, and his love for them knew no bounds. Riley had always shared a strong bond with my dad, while Lexi had grown closer to him during their time together in Helena.

My father's health began to deteriorate after he turned 80 years old. He was first diagnosed with prostate cancer, followed by Spinal Stenosis. Despite his health challenges, my father never complained or shared his struggles with anyone. As Riley underwent the transplant, my father's condition continued to worsen. His *Spinal Stenosis* progressed, and he suffered a fall that resulted in a broken hip. This happened while they were taking care of Lexi. Upon returning home, it was evident his declining health had significantly impacted him.

On November 11, 2007, it was evident that Papa was growing weary. It happened to be his 84th birthday, and all of us children came together to celebrate with him. That birthday became one of the most unforgettable moments we shared with him. He was cheerful, engaged in conversations, and simply relishing the precious moments spent with us. It felt like his final celebration—a grand farewell. Little did we know that it would indeed be the last time we would see him. Sadly, Papa contracted *pneumonia* and peacefully passed away at his home on December 17, 2007.

Mom later shared with us that she believed Dad held on until Riley received the transplant. She felt it was by the grace of God that he remained on this earth long enough to witness Riley with his new heart. With divine intervention, I truly believe he found the strength to stay with us just a little longer to savor moments with his family in good health.

The day following his passing, Riley awoke and recounted a dream he had. In his dream, he saw Papa and his other Grandpa Gus together in a warm, comforting place. Learning this brought me solace, knowing that Dad was at peace and reunited with Ron's father in the afterlife. I imagine they were raising a glass together, celebrating Riley's newfound health and happiness. It's a reminder that God's ways are truly mysterious.

Lexi's heart

Riley was thriving in high school and thoroughly enjoyed the experience. Observing his progress, I realized I could now shift some of my attention to Lexi. As an eighth-grader, she was relishing being back at school. However, she was still grappling with the fact that Riley had undergone a heart transplant, which weighed heavily on her mind. Whenever her heart raced or she felt unwell, she immediately jumped to the conclusion that there was something wrong with her heart. This led to her constantly questioning me about her cardiac health, displaying her deep-seated nervousness and fear of a similar fate befalling her. She was plagued by the notion that she, too, might require a heart transplant, a thought that filled her with dread. Despite our repeated explanations that Riley's heart condition was specific to his *DMD*, she remained highly anxious. To alleviate her concerns, I decided to take her to see her pediatrician to explore ways to ease her worries. After a thorough discussion about her fears regarding her heart, the doctor recommended an ultrasound to help reassure her and alleviate her anxiety.

She must have felt so insecure about her own body. What a scary feeling for her. You never know how your other children are going to react to such a distressing event in their lives. I was so glad I could calm her fears and worries about her own heart. I was always under the impression that I was acutely aware of how she was managing her life on a daily basis, but sometimes you drop the ball.

Lexi has always been an open-minded child, unafraid to speak her mind directly. Her brutal honesty sometimes felt like a wrecking ball, but I appreciated her candor when she opened up about how Riley's transplant was truly impacting her.

156

The day came for her to be tested, and the nurse took us into the waiting room. Without blinking, she looked at the orders, looked at Lexi, and then routinely asked if she was pregnant. Lexi was mortified! The look on her face was one of shock and disgust. After the initial shock of the question, Lexi answered with an emphatic "NO!" and I let out a small chuckle. This little incident broke the ice, and Lexi had her much-anticipated ultrasound. The results showed that Lexi had a perfectly healthy heart. She would not need a transplant and she definitely was not pregnant! She could put the worry about her own heart out of her mind and seemed glad to get out of the hospital after the mortifying question by the nurse.

I guess it should be no surprise that Lexi received a *Bachelor's Degree in Nursing* many years later.

> **Side Note for Parents:** Remember to always check in with your other children to see how they are coping with what is happening in their world. It is essential to reassure them that they can come to you if they have concerns about themselves. Their needs are just as important as the needs of the sick child. Life is like a balancing scale; sometimes, the scale is tipped because the needs of one person outweigh the needs of the other. Trying to even-the-scale-out is the tricky part.

Opportunity Knocks

"Opportunity knocks only once. You never know if you'll get another opportunity."[30]

When you think all of your prayers have been answered, God gives you another reason to have hope. Experiencing Riley's freshman year at Capital High School was wonderful. I would pick him and Lexi up from school and could be there for Riley at a moment's notice. Despite no longer being a preschool teacher, I found myself missing the social interactions that came with owning my own business. It felt like I was losing a part of myself. I had always been a mother, a wife, and a preschool teacher, and now one of those roles was gone. Letting go of the preschool felt like losing a family member. It had been a significant part of my life, and I loved being part of something larger than myself.

As a mother, there are times when you must make sacrifices for the ones you hold dear. Although you understand that your choices are for the greater good in the end, it doesn't lessen the pain of letting go of something you've dedicated your entire career to. Riley and Lexi essentially grew up in that preschool alongside the many children I had the pleasure of teaching. Lexi, in particular, spent so much time with me at the preschool that the staff affectionately dubbed her "The Little Principal." Like mother, like daughter.

Some of my best memories from their childhood were when I could bring them to work with me. It has truly been one of the greatest joys of my life. Little did I know that opportunity would again be knocking at my door.

It was December 2007 that I received a call from my friend Theresa. She asked if I would be interested in working 20 hours a week as a receptionist for the *Montana School Services Foundation* (*MSSF*). She had a friend who was looking to hire someone and Theresa told her I would be the perfect fit. I was nervous at the prospect of working again so soon after Riley's transplant. I said I would think about it. She gave me the number of the person to contact because they needed someone to start at the beginning of the new year.

That evening at the dinner table, I shared with everyone the unexpected job opportunity that had come my way. To my surprise, they were just as taken aback as I was, considering I had not planned on returning to work for at least a year. My top priority was ensuring everyone was adjusting well to our new normal, particularly Riley. Much to my astonishment, they all encouraged me to go ahead and interview for the position. Riley's only condition was that I would be there for him whenever he needed me, even if it meant dropping everything else. Despite feeling it was a long shot, I decided to go for the interview. I candidly explained my situation, and to my delight, they agreed to my terms. The individual who offered me the job was Pam Tudor, who has since become one of my closest and dearest friends. And just like that… I got my life back.

First Year Anniversary

At the first-year anniversary of Riley's transplant, I threw him a party to celebrate with family and friends. Riley doesn't like unwanted attention thrust upon him, but I felt we all needed a reason to come together to celebrate this magnificent milestone.

I distinctly remember Riley standing in the background, quietly mingling for the rest of the evening. Despite having gone through extraordinary circumstances, he prefers everything to be normal without any big fanfare. He didn't quite grasp why there was so much fuss. Looking back, I realize that the event was more for everyone else, as we all seek acknowledgment for our achievements. I felt that Riley, on the other hand, needed recognition for his survival. When his anniversary approaches now, we celebrate in a more low-key manner. We may go out for lunch or dinner, or I cook his favorite meal. These simple gestures are what he appreciates the most. It truly exemplifies the grace and humility that Riley possesses.

Lexi, Ron, Nina, Riley

We had a family picture taken that year. We hadn't had one since the kids were young, and I wanted to remember how Riley looked a year after almost dying. I still have the portrait sitting on our entertainment center. I keep it there so I can look at it every day and remember.

Driver's License

"Being challenged in life is inevitable, being defeated is optional."[31]

If you have a goal in mind, why not go for it? Reach for the stars. My family's favorite saying is, "There is no reason a disability should hold you back." They have always been a strong support system, full of love, care, and, most importantly, understanding.

Riley had a successful first year of high school, and as summer drew near, he brimmed with excitement. The approaching summer vacation meant he could enroll in Driver's Education, a huge accomplishment for him. Many boys with *DMD* never have the chance to experience the driver's seat, making this opportunity particularly meaningful for Riley. Despite the challenges, Riley remained physically capable of mastering driving skills independently. He could enter and exit the car unaided, steer confidently, control the gas and brake pedals effortlessly, and even easily perform necessary head checks.

At 15 years old, Riley was only 5 feet tall and weighed 110 lbs. He was considered short for his age, which was an advantage for someone with *DMD*. His lower weight meant he did not have to carry around as much on his weakened muscles. Ron and I believed that this factor helped slow down his disease progression. Since Riley did not experience a significant growth spurt, he was able to walk longer.

I remember when my brother Greg went through a growth spurt in high school. He grew rapidly and reached a height of 6 feet tall. However, due to this sudden growth, he often tripped and fell as his legs struggled to keep up with the rest of his body. Puberty also played a significant role in Greg's overall development.

Riley never went through puberty because he had been on Deflazacort since the age of 7 and a half. The medicine stunted his growth, so he had to consult an endocrinologist, who prescribed medication to help him transition through puberty. This was yet another challenging side effect of "The Beast," seeking its revenge. Despite "The Beast's" attempts to hinder him, Riley persevered and continued to move forward.

We credit *PPMD* and Pat Furlong for suggesting he be put on Deflazacort. Many parents of children with *DMD* were initially hesitant to consider steroid treatment for their sons, but those who did not opt for it saw their children transitioning to wheelchairs sooner due to muscle loss. We're grateful that we heeded Pat's advice!

Driver's education began immediately after the school year ended, and Riley was eager to dive in. He sat through classroom lectures on driver safety before moving on to the practical driving component of the course. Only Riley raised his hand when the driving instructor asked who wanted to take the wheel first. Ever since his heart transplant, he had been eagerly anticipating this moment, and nothing was going to hold him back from getting behind the wheel of the student driver's car.

When Riley went to sit in the car's driver's seat, the teacher noticed that Riley couldn't see over the steering wheel. I had already briefed the instructor about Riley's disability and how important it was to his independence that he drives. Without hesitation, the instructor went into the classroom and retrieved some books for Riley to sit on, enabling him to see over the dashboard and reach the pedals. And just like that... Riley drove a car for the first time.

When he got home, he was so jacked! He recounted the story to Ron and I in full detail. However, for the next driving session, we had to come up with an alternative to using books to prop him up. Riley had mentioned that the books kept sliding around, making it challenging for him to drive. Ron and I scoured every hardware store, box store, and nearly every retail outlet in Helena. Our final stop was at a retail store called Ross. With a sense of reluctance, Ron and I entered and embarked on our quest to find a suitable solution for Riley. We had to find something he could sit on and gain enough height to see over the steering wheel. We headed straight to the furniture section and stumbled upon a leather stool. After purchasing it and returning home, we successfully separated the leather seat from the stool legs, providing Riley with the necessary elevation for his upcoming driving lesson.

The next time he was scheduled to drive, I brought the leather seat and handed it to the instructor. The smile on his face let me know this was a great resolution to Riley's driving dilemma. The instructor told me he had hoped we could come up with something because he didn't want Riley to miss this important rite of passage as a teenager.

Riley successfully passed the class and obtained his Learner's Permit. The next milestone on his journey was to tackle the written and driving tests to obtain his official driver's license. Ron and I understood he couldn't continue driving around with a leather seat cushion indefinitely. It was essential for us to find a car that was tailored to his specific needs. After extensive online research and visiting every dealership in Helena, we finally discovered a suitable match for him -- a Toyota Yaris. This vehicle featured a unique design with the speedometer positioned in the center of the dashboard rather than behind the steering wheel. The moment Riley sat in the driver's seat of the little blue car, his face lit up with glee. Without hesitation, we decided to purchase the car right then and there. However, there was one adjustment we needed to make -- the seat needed to be able to move further up than the standard position allowed.

Ron and I often find ourselves in compromising situations regarding Riley. We are always brainstorming ways to ensure things work out for him. After purchasing the vehicle, I reached out to my close friend, Pam Tudor. Pam's husband, Dave Tudor, owns Tudor Machine Shop, and I believed he could assist us. We brought the car to his shop, where he skillfully modified the seat to enable Riley to drive his new vehicle. Thank God for good friends.

In December, Ron accompanied Riley to the DMV, where he successfully passed the written and driving tests. His steadfast persistence had finally paid off. God was shining a light on Riley that day. When he got home, the smile on his face could have lit up the whole room. I like to think a little intervention was involved that day, especially when he passed the parallel parking portion of the test! Maybe, just maybe, it was all part of God's plan.

With a newly minted driver's license in his hand and a Toyota Yaris to proudly drive, Riley's inaugural road trip was to Great Falls, Montana, where he would spend the weekend with his uncles, Greg and Dave. This journey marked the beginning of many solo adventures that Riley would embark on throughout his high school years and beyond. Isn't Life Grand?

After obtaining his driver's license, I talked to the high school principal to discuss a parking arrangement for Riley. *Capital High* generously granted Riley a designated parking space at the rear of the school. Additionally, a ramp by the back entrance made it more convenient for Riley to access his car and reduced the distance to the school. Once again, Walt came through for Riley, providing him with this urgently required lifeline. This new arrangement meant that Riley could now enjoy the typical high school experience of having a car like any other student.

Riley, Age 16

One of the problems we faced with the parking space at the high school was the harsh winter conditions. We couldn't risk Riley not being able to drive because his parking spot wasn't cleared of snow. Ron believed in being proactive in such situations. Consequently, Ron would prepare his shovel and winter gear whenever there was a significant snowfall. He would arrive at the school before anyone else and clear the snow from the four designated parking spaces at the back. Ron was determined to ensure that all those spots were accessible. He performed this selfless deed for his son without seeking recognition. Ron continued to shovel those spaces until the day Riley graduated.

Chico, The Emotional Support Rescue Dog

In August 2008, Chico arrived at the Lewis and Clark Humane Society in Helena, Montana, and would change our lives forever.

Riley and Lexi had wanted a dog for a very long time. We had many discussions about this topic and Ron and I always felt we should wait until they were old enough to share the responsibility. We decided to fulfill their long-held dream of adopting a dog a year after Riley's transplant.

Miraculously, Riley received his new heart on March 31, 2007. After a year of acclimating to his new heart, the promise of a dog would be achieved.

163

Our niece, Stefanie Herrera, worked at the *Lewis and Clark Humane Society*, and we had her on the lookout for a small dog. We received a phone call from her informing us that a Chihuahua Terrier was available for rescue. We went down that very day and adopted him. We all agreed on the name Chico. We were told Chico was two years old and abandoned in the Applebee's parking lot. His misfortune tuned out to be our

Chico & Riley

fortune. From the very moment we brought him home, he slept on Riley's bed. As Riley's disease continued to progress, Chico was there as Riley's much-needed comfort and companionship.

Chico would wait on Riley's bed every morning as he got ready for the day. He would then ride Riley's wheelchair around the house. This daily ritual brought much happiness and joy. Chico sat right next to Riley as they enjoyed their meal together.

Chico's story poignantly reminds us of the extraordinary bond between humans and animals. His arrival at the right moment, during a period of immense transition, irrevocably transformed all our lives. As Chico celebrates his 18th birthday, he stands as a symbol of hope, resilience, and the enduring power of companionship.

Ultimately, he rescued all of us and is still with us today.

The Transplant Letter

The only information we ever received about Riley's heart transplant donor was that it came from a small adult. All other details are kept confidential unless the donor's family chooses to initiate contact with the recipient. Following the first-year anniversary of the transplant, recipients are permitted to compose a letter to the donor's family. However, it is entirely optional for the recipient to decide whether they wish to do so. The letter is conveyed through the transplant coordinator.

It had been 18 months since the transplant we sat down with Riley and made the decision to write to the donor's family. Riley believed it was important to express our gratitude. He wanted to convey how significantly the transplant had transformed his quality of life.

Here's the letter:

On March 31, 2007, Riley received a very special gift. He received the gift of a new heart and a new lease on life. His new heart was a simple gesture of your loved one checking the YES box to be a donor. This gesture of complete selflessness saved my son's life, and we will forever be grateful. If someone were to ask me to sum up Riley's journey in three short sentences, they would be this: Boy needs heart. Boy gets heart. The boy lives happily ever after. Life, however, isn't ever that simple.

When Riley was 10 years old, he was diagnosed with a condition that weakens the heart muscle. He was put on medications to improve his heart function, and for 4 years, those medicines worked great. Then, in January of 2007, at a routine checkup in Billings, things went terribly wrong. The cardiologist came in and told us that Riley's heart was no longer functioning properly and that the only solution would be for him to have a heart transplant. Riley was airlifted to *Cincinnati Children's Hospital.* There, he was put on a waiting list to receive a new heart. Riley received the best possible medical care until his new heart arrived. On a beautiful spring day in March of 2007, we received a call that would change our lives forever. A perfect heart for Riley was available. A team of doctors came in and was ready to take Riley away. I remember telling him that everything was going to be ok because the next time we saw him, he would have a new heart and a new outlook on life.

The next time we saw Riley after the surgery, we could already see a difference. He had color back in his cheeks and looked more vital and full of life than we had seen him in years. His grayish color skin was gone, and his energy level increased dramatically. He used to come home from school and be so tired that he barely made it through the day. With his new heart, however, he immediately started to breathe better, and his stamina started to come back. He told us right after the surgery, that he could actually breathe. His body had gotten so used to his old heart that it didn't know how it felt to actually take a good deep breath.

After the transplant, Riley was able to start his freshman year at Capital High along with the rest of his class. This past summer, he took Driver's Ed and will be receiving his license in December. None of this would have ever been possible if your loved one hadn't decided to be a donor.

So, thank you for making the decision to honor your loved one's choice. My son is a living example of your loved one's unbelievable generosity to pass on the gift of life.

Thank you.

I have a wall-hanging in my house that says, "Every cloud has a silver lining." Our cloud was Riley needing a heart transplant, and the silver lining was the donor.

Unfortunately, we have never heard back from the donor's family. I understand that it might have been too painful for them to reach out to us. Sometimes, things are better left alone. Ron and I thank God every day for the amazing gift they bestowed upon Riley. I hope they have found comfort and solace in the last 16 years because I know we have.

High School Years

Riley continued walking through high school while enjoying the newfound freedom behind the wheel of his new car. He continued to travel to Cincinnati for his heart checkups. We were fortunate to arrange interim care for Riley in Spokane, Washington, as Montana lacks a transplant team. Riley needed to make the trip every six months. Since Spokane was approximately five hours away, we turned these journeys into mini vacations for Riley and Lexi. We aimed to travel as a family whenever our schedules permitted. In instances when Lexi and I couldn't join, Ron would take Riley to watch the Gonzaga Bulldogs basketball team. This team was one of Riley's favorite college basketball teams, and it provided him with something to anticipate eagerly.

Riley's Senior Portrait

Riley thoroughly appreciated his high school experience due to the supportive group of friends who accepted him for who he was, his disability, and all. He was fortunate not to face any bullying, and his terminal disease was not prominently noticeable, aside from his use of the elevator and the additional time he required for tests. The way *Capital High* accommodated Riley left us impressed. He couldn't have gone to a better high school.

Graduation Day!!

One of the biggest achievements in anybody's life is walking down the aisle and receiving your high school diploma. Riley's high school years went by so fast that it seemed like it was all a dream. If you had told me my son was going to WALK to get his high school diploma, I would have told you to pinch me because I wouldn't have believed it was real.

A few weeks before graduation, I contacted the vice-principal, Walt Chancy, to speak with him about the logistics of Riley walking to receive his diploma. There were two scenarios involved in this process.

First, they would have the ceremony outside on the football field if weather permitted.

Second, if perhaps the weather was disagreeable, it would be held inside the gym.

I could tell Walt had spent a lot of time and effort making sure Riley would walk without a hitch.

Riley couldn't use a folding chair to sit in because it was too low for him to be able to push himself up out of it. He refused to be helped that day. He wanted to do this on his own. Riley always knew his limits. He tried several chairs, and they found one that would work. Walt also made sure we were allowed to drop Riley off very close to where the ceremony would take place so he didn't have to walk far. We will never forget the kindness and generosity Walt showed Riley. He was truly remarkable throughout Riley's high school years.

Graduation arrived on a beautiful, sunny, warm June day. It felt as though God's light was shining down on all of us. Witnessing

Riley Walking at Graduation

Riley rise from his chair, walk confidently across the stage, and receive his diploma was truly moving. Ron and I felt overwhelming pride as we watched our son achieve this milestone. Each time Riley accomplished something he was told he might never do, it served as a reminder of how extraordinary he is. Riley has never ceased to amaze us. He still does to this day!

I wouldn't wish this disease on my worst enemy. It can consume your whole life if you let it. My advice is simple: don't let it! Find joy and wonder in the little accomplishments, and savor the big ones because they will last a lifetime. Look for things to celebrate and be happy as your child grows and develops. Relive those precious memories with them. Remind them of their uniqueness every day and teach them to take pride in their achievements, no matter their size. Ron and I often reminisce with Riley about the good old days, but we always look forward to the new adventures to come.

It Takes a Village

It takes a village to raise a child, but in our unique situation, it took a village (community) to SAVE THE CHILD!

In Riley's journey, it wasn't just one village, but many: *PPMD*, *CCH*, Early Movement Preschool, family, friends, Rossiter Elementary, C.R. Anderson Middle School, Capital High, the Helena community, the transplant team, and countless doctors, both past and present. These distinct communities united with a singular purpose: to support and save Riley.

As Riley grew older, the village evolved, becoming smaller yet remaining just as significant. We have all carried Riley on our shoulders at one time or another.

Too Cold To Handle

Dealing with "The Beast" isn't for the faint of heart. It requires a willingness to go the extra mile to ensure your child can survive and thrive. This was just one of the many occasions when Ron and I found ourselves in a predicament like this. The decision itself wasn't difficult to make; rather, the intricate details involved proved to be troublesome.

169

Riley's first two years at college in Helena took a toll on him, culminating in a problematic last semester. It was a truly cold winter. During this time, Riley experienced increasing stiffness in his hands, accompanied by numbness and trembling exacerbated by the cold weather. His feet, too, were constantly cold, making it increasingly difficult for him to navigate the snowy terrain. The icy conditions posed an additional hazard, often causing him to slip and fall, requiring assistance to get back on his feet.

We were confronted yet again with the parking issue. This time however, the college would not oblige our request for a personal parking space for Riley. We would always hold our breath when he left because we never knew if he would find an available space amongst the ones Ron had shoveled. The first time he missed class due to not finding a shoveled space marked the end of that uncertainty. I would follow Riley to school and shovel another space if all the ones Ron previously shoveled were taken. I know this may sound extreme, and you may be thinking to yourself, "Why didn't we just drive him to school on those days? It would be so much easier for all of you." We like to take the road that is less traveled. Why should Riley have to sacrifice not being able to drive because it might take a little extra time out of our busy day? That was our perspective on things. He should be able to drive to school come hell or high water. We were there to make sure that happened. That's one of the many reasons why I love Ron so much! He was always looking for ways to let Riley live like a normal human being. He wouldn't allow Riley to think he was anything less. Thanks for being there for Riley.

Riley's history of falls extends back to his childhood. He wore an ankle brace because his legs would give out for no apparent reason, and he would sprain his ankle. A particularly serious incident resulted in a fractured tailbone, along with multiple compression fractures in his back, significantly impacting his overall health.

We remember a frightening incident when Riley was back in high school. His class at Capital High required him to leave the main building and walk across the parking lot to attend a class held in a separate building.

170

It was 20 degrees below zero that day, and the parking lot was slick with ice. Riley found himself alone, the last person out of that class. As he made his way through the icy parking lot, he slipped and was unable to get back up. Despite his screams, no one seemed to hear him.

God must have been watching out for Riley that day because his friend Coltan appeared after lying on the ground for some time. Coltan found Riley lying flat on his back, shivering in the cold. He picked him up and brought him to his car. Interestingly, Coltan later revealed that he had never walked that way before; he simply chose a different route to get to class that day. It's chilling to think about what could have happened otherwise. Little miracles happen every day.

Montana State of Mind

It was becoming abundantly clear that if Riley wanted to still keep walking, we would have to relocate to warmer weather. Where to move, where to move? That was the million-dollar question. Ron and I had become accustomed to these kinds of situations, and as always, Riley's needs had to come first. We would deal with the rest of the fallout later. We needed to move somewhere close enough so that family could visit.

We also decided that having family living in one of these warmer climates would be ideal. Moving to Las Vegas, Nevada, seemed like the best solution. My brother Chris lived in Henderson, Nevada, and my nephew Robert lived in Vegas. Chris had always taken care of my brothers, and I knew that if any situation arose where we needed help, he would be the one to come to the rescue. One thing I knew for sure about Chris was that you could always count on him. My nephew Robert was an added bonus. Robert was my sister Maria's only child, and I practically grew up with him since we were only 11 years apart. He felt more like a little brother to me.

We moved to Henderson, Nevada, in 2013 because we could no longer tolerate "The Beast" wreaking havoc in our lives. It manifested through a multitude of issues for Riley, pushing us to our breaking point. We refused to let it claim another piece of Riley's essence, particularly his cherished ability to walk.

We would make the best of the ordeal because we knew Riley wanted this. We decided to move in May because Riley was just finishing his second year of college. We sold the handicap-equipped house that we had so lovingly built for Riley.

Ron was able to take a voluntary transfer with his job and was relocated to the Las Vegas Division. I resigned from my position at *MSSF*, and Lexi had just completed her first year at Montana State University. She graciously assisted us with the move and planned to stay for the summer break. Ron and I had already visited Vegas twice in search of a suitable home. Chris played a pivotal role in connecting us with a realtor and accompanied us on house-hunting expeditions. Eventually, we managed to purchase a spec house that was still under construction. We made arrangements to customize the house to ensure it was handicap accessible. Following a month of living in a condo, we finally moved into our new home. We all embraced our new lifestyle in Henderson, Nevada. We knew we were trying to run away from "The Beast," and for a short while, it worked. It seemed like he couldn't find us, and then BAM!

Riley was 22 years old when we relocated to Henderson, Nevada. Prior to our move, he used to drive a car. However, within a year of our relocation, his ability to drive ended abruptly. Riley found himself unable to lift his foot from the gas pedal to apply the brakes. Additionally, he suffered a fall on his way to the pool, resulting in permanent nerve damage in his right leg. Riley never allowed these setbacks to defeat him.

One of his ambitions upon moving to Nevada was to complete his college education. Riley had enrolled at Nevada State University, opting for this institution over UNLV due to its smaller campus, which would be more manageable for him considering his limited mobility. With Riley unable to walk long distances or drive, I took on the role of his full-time chauffeur.

"The Beast" took away his independence, and he now relied on others to care for him. How much more can he endure? Despite facing a terminal illness, he continued to fight, refusing to let it overpower him. His incredible bravery is truly unbelievable.

When traveling by plane, Riley utilized a portable mobility scooter due to the long nature of airport concourses. He made the decision to incorporate the scooter into his campus routine for getting around. However, we understood this was merely a temporary solution, as we knew what was lurking around the corner.

Ron refers to *Duchenne Muscular Dystrophy* as "The Disease of Fire." Since our relocation to Nevada, the intense heat had been sapping Riley's energy. Despite his increased water intake, he experienced edema in his legs, causing them to tighten and cramp. A clear progression that was leading to another major life-changing condition in Riley's life.

When it rains, it pours! A year after we moved, Riley would make the transition into the wheelchair. He took this a lot better than me. I think he felt a sigh of relief because, in the end, the struggle to continue walking wasn't worth the damage it was doing to his body. We couldn't believe his disease had progressed that fast in such a short period of time. Again, we were fooled. We only moved because we wanted Riley to have the independence he so craved, and those cold Montana winters weren't helping. In the end, the heat proved to be too much. Riley lost that battle, but he never let it get him down.

Drug Holiday

Riley was prescribed testosterone and growth hormone at age 15 due to his hypothyroidism resulting from *DMD*. Following the transplant, he was also put on Prednisone as per the *CCH* protocol, which required him only to use FDA-approved drugs. As Deflazacort was not *FDA*-approved, he had to switch to Prednisone, which initially raised concerns due to its potentially nasty side effects. Despite our worries, Riley responded well to the Prednisone treatment. We believe that the combination of testosterone and growth hormone may have played a role in mitigating the adverse effects of Prednisone, ultimately contributing to Riley's positive response to the medication.

After a conference call with his doctor, he suggested Riley take a drug holiday as he had been on growth hormone and testosterone. Given that he was now 23, it seemed like a good idea to try weaning him off these

173

medications for a little while. Following their advice, we discontinued Riley's testosterone and growth hormone treatment. Within three months, Riley underwent a dramatic transformation. He experienced a significant weight gain of 20 lbs. and developed a moon face due to an increased appetite. He became increasingly agitated quickly, and his patience with us was wearing thin. The most alarming change was that he was starting to lose muscle function rapidly. He was having a hard time eating on his own and couldn't even pick up a water bottle. He was becoming weaker by the day. It was evident that he was deteriorating before our eyes. Upon checking his levels, it was confirmed they were very low and far from optimal. Without delay, Riley's doctor reinstated his crucial medications. Subsequently, Riley began to show immediate signs of improvement. Furthermore, he was permitted to resume Deflazacort after it had received *FDA* approval.

Ron and I strongly believe that Riley's use of Testosterone, growth hormone, and Deflazacort played an important role in enabling him to walk into his 20s and maintain high functionality. Several months later, Riley returned to his usual self. He shed the excess weight, his temperament mellowed, and he started eating regular meals independently. Nevertheless, he still had to rely on a wheelchair. The irreversible damage had already been done.

I cried almost every day for a long time when Riley started using a wheelchair. I couldn't talk about it because every time I tried, I would have a panic attack. I couldn't bring myself to tell anyone because my emotions overwhelmed me. Riley didn't deserve this, especially after all the challenges he has already faced. When life knocks him down, he powers through like a bulldozer. He's my hero!

Riley continued to progress at Nevada State University, becoming more accustomed to living in a wheelchair. While reliant on a wheelchair for mobility, Riley retained the ability to walk with assistance during transitions to his bed or recliner. With the support of Ron and myself, Riley walked with assistance until age 25, a remarkable feat for individuals with

DMD. Riley consistently challenges the limits imposed on *DMD* patients, pushing beyond expectations for boys with this condition.

Now that Riley was confined to a wheelchair, the idea of moving back home became more and more enticing. We felt a strong sense of belonging to Montana. When we relocated to Nevada, I was responsible for helping everyone adjust to a new home, job, and college. Ron had dedicated 25 years to his job, and the prospect of retirement was becoming more appealing by the day. After discussing it with Riley, we decided that he would complete his college degree at Nevada State. We all agreed on this plan because Riley was so close to finishing, and we didn't want anything to hinder his progress. Riley was able to accomplish his dream of graduating from Nevada State University. In December 2017, Riley received his Bachelor of Arts (BA) in Criminal Justice and a minor in Psychology. Take that *DMD*!

When we relocated to Nevada, Chris was always there to assist in any way he could. He also provided much-needed companionship for Riley when he required a friend. Chris would frequently take him out for dinner and to the movies, and he would often come over to our house to watch sporting events with him. My nephew Robert also played a significant role in Riley's life, and to this day, they share a strong bond that continues to endure.

They were sad to see us leave Henderson but knew our hearts were in Montana. We were relieved to escape the intense heat, which appeared to be a significant factor in Riley's progression into the wheelchair. I am confident they would be there in a heartbeat if I ever needed anything. That's just how our family operates. When we got back to Helena, they both come up once a year to visit with us and other family members.

In just four short years, we were back in Helena, Mt., and we never looked back; God has a way of leading us in the right direction. The Last Best Place never looked so good! When you're facing "The Beast," all you see is darkness. Only when you regain control do you start to glimpse the light. Over the years, we have gathered the necessary survival tools to confront any challenge head-on. Acquiring these tools has been a journey filled with numerous experiences and lessons.

Despite the darkness, we have encountered moments of brightness and joy. We cherish these happy times and look forward to creating many more. Once again, we find comfort in that powerful word—HOPE!

Back Where We Belong

There's no place like home; to us, that home is in Montana. Over our 32 years of marriage, Ron and I have resided in five different homes, three of which were specifically designed to be handicap accessible. When we share this with others, they often assume we are in the business of flipping houses. However, every time we embarked on building a new home, we always had Riley in mind. This consideration for Riley's needs continued when we made the decision to move back to Montana. Despite our search, we couldn't find a suitable home that would cater to our requirements. Whenever we found a potential option, it always turned out that extensive renovations were needed, making the idea of building a custom home from the ground up a more practical and cost-effective choice. So, once again, we built a house, and we continue to reside in it today.

Riley was eager to secure a job and integrate into the Helena community. Being physically challenged can sometimes be seen as a disadvantage. He can only work for a few hours a day due to his physical limitations, not because of any mental challenges. This misconception is a common mistake people often make. They assume that just because he uses a wheelchair, he may not be able to meet the job's requirements. This assumption is simply not true!

Riley had never been employed before, so he decided to explore opportunities in customer service. However, after facing multiple rejections from large retailers due to his inability to lift 50 lbs., Riley's enthusiasm began to wane. He yearned to find a place where he belonged, but the growing belief that his disability was a barrier left him feeling increasingly disheartened.

Ron and I recently joined a fitness club that is part of a national chain. After becoming acquainted with the manager, I approached her about

176

the possibility of hiring Riley. Despite informing her about Riley's disability, she showed no hesitation. Interestingly, they were in need of a part-time staff member, so they encouraged Riley to submit an application. Following a successful interview, Riley commenced work the following week. He was thrilled with this opportunity as he enjoys interacting with people and working at the front desk provided him with the perfect outlet to integrate into his work routine. He was getting back into the swing of things.

Things were going well for the first seven months, but when the regional manager visited the facility, he was unimpressed with Riley's performance. He believed Riley was not meeting the expectations outlined in the handbook. The manager began introducing new physical tasks that Riley struggled to complete, leading to criticism. Over time, Riley felt increasingly diminished by the regional manager's actions. Seven months had gone by, and Riley's work performance was outstanding. Now it all looked inevitable that Riley would suffer consequences at the hands of this idiot.

Next, he reduced Riley's hours from four days a week to just two. Riley felt extremely frustrated that such a change was permitted. In this modern day and age, one would expect people to be more tolerant and understanding. I discussed the situation with the manager, who shared our disillusionment. Despite the manager's efforts to reason with the individual in charge, Riley's hours continued to be cut without consideration. It was an understatement to say that Riley was experiencing discrimination. The final blow came when Riley was informed that his hours were further reduced to only one day a week, leaving him feeling furious when he returned home.

I stepped in and decided to take matters into my own hands. I attempted to contact corporate without success. Subsequently, I acquired the Regional Manager's phone number and reached out to him directly. I was clearly deeply upset by the situation, but he responded brusquely and showed no empathy. He seemed disinterested in hearing my perspective, and his stance was final. Following this interaction, Riley resigned the following day under considerable duress. We would later find out that this Regional Manager was fired for incompetency. This incident would leave a sour taste in our mouths for a long time.

No matter what you do to Riley, he will never give up. That lit a fire in him. He turned to Vocational Rehabilitation, and they were able to help him find a job using his degree. Riley continues to work part-time for the *Department of Justice* for the State of Montana.

Sometimes, we cherish the small victories because they prepare us to handle the larger problems that truly matter. In moments when the little triumphs slip away, leaving room for the significant ones to take center stage, it becomes essential to find humor amid hardships to prevent being consumed by sorrow.

Riley isn't seeking charity but rather a helping hand to achieve success. His experiences with a heart transplant, *Duchenne's* disease, and everyday life exist in distinct compartments. Trying to grapple with all these aspects simultaneously would overwhelm him, as each one carries its own weight of trauma. This compartmentalization is his survival mechanism, a way to navigate through life's complexities while preserving his well-being. Fortunately, Ron and I have been able to offer our support and manage various aspects of his life.

Reflecting on his past, Riley shared, "When I was 14, thoughts of death never crossed my mind. At that age, you're not supposed to contemplate mortality." I thank GOD every day for the dedicated efforts of the medical professionals, advocates like Pat Furlong, and the generous organ donor because at just 14 years old, it was not Riley's time to depart from this world.

The first few years back home were incredibly hectic, to say the least. It was a period of significant adjustment for all of us. Despite being back in familiar territory, life seemed to be in constant flux. Through it all, we have learned to adapt to whatever curveballs life has thrown our way. With faith and hope that we had made the right choice, we pressed forward, one step at a time.

When Riley turned 25, he still needed assistance to walk. One afternoon, as I was helping him transfer from his wheelchair to his favorite recliner, his right leg suddenly buckled. I still had my hands around his waist because I had just helped him up from his chair. It felt like we were moving in slow motion as he fell. Time seemed to slow down as he descended. I instinctively took the brunt of his weight and ended up coming down with him to cushion his fall. He came down, landing on top of me. Thankfully, we were both okay, but the snapping sound his leg made upon impact was horrifying, to say the least.

After climbing out from underneath him, I assessed the situation. Riley was in too much pain for me to move him alone. I immediately called Ron, who rushed home to help. Together, we managed to get Riley to his bed, where he remained for two days. Despite his reluctance, Riley refused to go to the hospital. However, after struggling for hours on the third day to get him to sit up and put weight on his right leg, I knew we had to call in the big guns.

Riley started feeling nauseous, causing increasing concern among us. Uncle Buddy (Dave), who had faced a similar situation in the past, urged Riley to go to the emergency room as he suspected a possible femur fracture based on his own experience. Unable to move Riley ourselves, we had no choice but to call for an ambulance.

Once he was assessed in the emergency room and a broken femur was confirmed, we faced a pivotal decision. The local hospital determined that they were unable to perform surgery on him due to his *DMD*. They recommended airlifting him to Spokane, Washington. However, aware of the presence of qualified doctors in Great Falls, Montana, I informed the ER doctor that if Great Falls declined to admit him, he could be airlifted to Spokane. After consulting with the medical team, the doctor informed us that Riley would be transported by ambulance to Benefis Hospital in Great Falls, MT. This news brought us immense relief, and we followed behind the ambulance as it made its way to the hospital. Throughout the ordeal, we stayed with Dave and Greg until Riley underwent the surgery and was eventually discharged to return home. Once again, God has taken us under His wing.

Once we returned home, the real healing process began. Riley realized that breaking his femur meant the end of his walking days completely, which was another tough pill to swallow. We had to arrange for home health services to come in and teach us how to transfer Riley using a lift. This was a challenging task that required adjustment from Riley, Ron, and me.

Ron was able to take some time off from his new "post-retirement job" to help me adjust to taking care of Riley. Even after Ron went back to work, I still felt shaky about caring for Riley by myself. Breaking a femur is a significant challenge for anyone, and even more so for someone with *DMD*. I knew I needed to seek assistance. My sister Maria lived just outside of town by Canyon Ferry Lake. When I explained to her what kind of a pickle I was in, she offered to help without hesitation. She worked in town and her boss allowed her to come over on her lunch break and assist me in getting Riley ready for the day. After six weeks of continuous care, I finally felt confident to care for Riley independently. Maria's positive attitude and humor provided much-needed relief during this stressful time. Her kindness and love for Riley will never be forgotten.

Nine Lives

I witnessed Riley's life flash before my eyes many times, and each time, the outcome left me astonished. I truly believe God had a special plan for Riley -- a plan that was to live! Ron and I affectionately referred to Riley as "El Gato," the cat, because we swear to God he has nine lives.

Riley's 9 lives:

1 Diagnosed at three with terminal disease (*DMD*): still proving everybody wrong
2 Put on steroids at seven-and-a-half years old: still on them today
3 Told he would be in a wheelchair at 10: went into a wheelchair at 23
4 Told he would be dead at 17: still living at 31

5   Diagnosed with Cardiomyopathy at 10: put on life-saving medication

6   Heart failure at 14

7   Received lifesaving transplant at 14

8   Seizure after transplant and given last rites: he miraculously pulls through yet again

9   Walked until he was 25 with support

Every time Riley faced these nine challenges, it felt as though death was knocking at our door. However, during these moments, Riley would bring his "A game." Despite facing seemingly insurmountable odds, Riley has achieved remarkable feats, defying expectations and overcoming each brush with mortality. In these critical moments, it seemed as though a divine power was guiding Riley through. Ron and I also held steadfast faith in our doctors, trusting in their expertise and dedication each time we entrusted Riley's care to them. With these two entities working in tandem, Riley has achieved remarkable success in conquering every obstacle that has crossed his path.

30th Birthday

Turning 30 is a big deal, but to Riley, it was gargantuan. Here he was, turning 30 years old with *DMD* and 15 years rejection-free from his heart transplant. TWO huge milestones in the same year were hard to believe. We wanted to do something special to mark these magnificent occasions. Riley decided he wanted to take a trip to Vegas to mark this monumental occasion.

Logistically, it would prove to be a nightmare. Greg and Dave accompanied us, which meant we needed to find two completely handicap-accessible rooms. The ideal rooms would have an electric track system on the ceiling and electric beds. The track system runs from the bed to the bathroom, and you just need a sling to support the person being transferred. Dave searched through every website to find rooms in Las Vegas until he came across Wynn and Encore, which had two rooms available that met our requirements. The beds were electric, just like the one Riley had at home. Finding such specific rooms can be challenging, so we were fortunate they had two available. Greg and Dave rarely traveled because of the effort involved, especially as they got older, and it became harder on their bodies. They agreed to join us on this trip because it was for Riley. They wouldn't have missed it for anything in the world.

Others joining us for his celebration included Lexi, her fiancé Nick, my sister Maria, her boyfriend Bill, my nephew Robert, his wife Brittany, and one of Riley's best friends, Brian. It was going to be a family affair as we planned to throw Riley the BLOW OUT birthday party he truly deserved.

Since my brother Chris still lived in the area, he organized a family dinner at a local Italian restaurant. We had a fantastic time celebrating Riley's 30 years of life.

Before our big trip to Vegas, we had another surprise for Riley. We threw him a surprise party at a local brewery in town and invited all of Riley's friends and family. He had no idea and was genuinely surprised. Everyone had a fantastic time, and it was a birthday celebration that will be remembered for years to come!

Reflections

Riley, Lexi, Ron, and I have learned much from what I call Greg and Dave's playbook. The playbook could be titled "How to Survive Life with a Terminal Disease." They have been a great source of inspiration for us and continue to inspire us today. Without their support and guidance, we would not be where we are today.

Upon further reflection, Greg and Dave shared their thoughts as I wrapped up my interview with them.

Dave reflected, "We had *SMA* together. It was a unique situation; two family members were going through the same challenges. In many ways, we were fortunate because we could rely on each other for support. Our bond was indescribable and served as our driving force, although most people couldn't comprehend it."

I replied, "Yeah, it did allow you guys to bond. I think one thing that happened was your character; you were no longer Uncle Dave but became known as Uncle Buddy. You came forward and made sure everybody got what they needed. In times of stress, the family looked for someone who understood. That became Uncle Buddy."

Curious about the role of faith in their resilience, I inquired, "Do you believe that your faith and identity provided you with that additional strength and determination?"

Greg pondered, "Perhaps many individuals possess that inner strength, only realizing it when faced with adversity. In challenging moments, having each other to lean on becomes crucial. I certainly found solace in that."

Dave chimed in, "Yeah, and I think we believed in each other and the three of us (Greg, Dave and Riley), in a wheelchair. The bond between us is a bond that nobody else will ever understand. It's a bond that will always be there. Riley knows and everybody knows he's got his parents, but we're always there for him. It's always this bond that will never be broken. I believe faith has something to do with it. Mom and Dad always said, 'You're not better than anybody, but nobody's better than you.'"

Reflecting on their upbringing, Greg shared, "Our parents strived to maintain a sense of normalcy. While I couldn't participate in certain physical activities like others, I found joy in pursuits such as hunting and fishing."

Dave stated, "We had a big family and lots of friends living in town who were part of the faith too. We grew up with cousins who would do a lot with us. There were times when they would throw us in the boat to go fishing, and they were willing to do the hard work to have us with them. They didn't even think about how hard it was to get us into the boat."

Greg reflected, "We were very imperfect people; we struggled with life a lot, and things weren't always the greatest. You can't sugarcoat our life. We all made our share of mistakes, but we survived. We care for each other, and we are good people despite our mistakes. I will fight for family. We are willing to help if we can. Our faith helped us through all of this, and we are far from perfect. There's always somebody worse off than you. Then came our nephew Riley, who had it worse than us. We were thinking we had to have the same thing and so did everybody else."

Adding to the conversation, Dave remarked, "Our upbringing instilled in us a strong faith that we could weather any storm that came our way. Our family always approached challenges with the belief that we had the resilience to overcome them, no matter how daunting."

I interjected, "But unlike you guys, Riley faced medical issues that you never had to contend with. Given your spinal muscular atrophy, were you prescribed any medications or receiving injections at the time?"

Dave responded, "Back then, there weren't any treatments available for what we were dealing with."

Greg recalled, "There wasn't any so-called medical intervention that I can recall."

Continuing the discussion, I pointed out, "So, the only form of care you received was primarily physical, involving the use of braces, wheelchairs, commodes, walkers, and canes. It seems like there wasn't much scientific advancement in that regard at the time."

Dave confirmed, "That's correct."

Greg added, "Yeah, but they were working on things all the time. Today, they can do a lot more when the boys are young. In utero, they can detect *SMA* and DMD.

I noted, "Indeed, early intervention can make a significant difference in managing SMA."

Dave elaborated, "Yes, although we are older now, the impact is not the same as it would be on a younger person. We do take a liquid medication that is intended to slow down the progression of the condition. However, age remains a factor in how effective it can be."

Greg shared, "We're in our late fifties and early sixties, constantly seeking anything to help us maintain our strength. The medication we're currently taking plays a critical role in preserving what little strength we have left. It enables me to perform simple tasks like lifting my hand to play poker or picking up a mug or a bottle of water."

When asked about his experience, Dave expressed, "I still drive a handicap van and live with my brother. The medication helps me maintain my current abilities, and I haven't experienced any worsening in the past couple of years. It seems to have halted or slowed down any potential progression of my condition. That's the impact it has had on us."

I said, "So, right now, that has helped you. But there is nothing out there like that for *DMD*. Riley has *Duchenne Muscular Dystrophy*, which is even worse because it's terminal. All muscular dystrophies are terminal, but Riley's has been terminal since he was three."

When asked about his diagnosis, Greg shared, "The doctors were uncertain, mentioning that reaching 36 years old could be considered a significant milestone."

Dave added, "I didn't undergo the extensive testing and procedures like Greg did to uncover the root cause of our condition. Our parents were already familiar with managing the situation, so I simply followed suit. We embraced the uncertainty, determined to make the most of our circumstances and maintain as much normalcy as possible."

My brothers told Riley that you determine your own fate, not anybody else. Riley has always possessed a strong spirit. Growing up with Greg and Dave in wheelchairs, he has never known them any other way. Our family's unique life experience has enabled Riley to understand what to expect, what it feels like to be disabled, and how to live with it. Greg and Dave taught him that being in a wheelchair doesn't signify the end of your life.

When Riley turned eighteen, Greg and Dave assisted us in accessing the benefits that Riley was entitled to as an adult. Their support was invaluable.

Greg explained, "We taught you how to maneuver the system so that you could identify all the resources available for families of disabled people if expenses were prohibitive. It's not just wheelchairs and stuff that's covered through your insurance, but it's the cost of getting a handicap adaptable or a retrofitted Van. They could run tens of thousands of dollars on top of the purchase price."

Back: Lexi, Maria, Robert, Mom, Nina, Ron
Front: Greg, Dave, Riley

I responded, "It's important that people know what's available out there and how they can access it. Money is often in short supply and you guys helped us navigate that when we started to need the equipment."

Greg reminded me, "We located that van for you in Missoula," while Dave chimed in, "We urged you to act quickly to have the equipment installed. For many, even affording the van itself is a challenge."

Greg continued, reflecting on the financial aspect, "Funding was available at that time, whereas many others struggle to afford such necessities."

Grateful for their assistance, I acknowledged, "Yes, I remember we had to purchase a van first, and then there was funding to install adaptive equipment. You guys helped us. Otherwise, it would have been a struggle for us. Without your help, sorting out what we needed would have been a hard time. It took us some years to be able to identify everything available to us. By the time we needed some of this equipment, we had much more information and knew how to navigate through to get them."

Today, Greg and Dave remain in Great Falls, playing an essential role in our lives. Their continued support inspires me, and I am thankful for their presence during both the highs and lows. I truly couldn't have managed my life with Riley without them.

Expert Reflections

Pat Furlong, Founding President and CEO of *Parent Project Muscular Dystrophy (PPMD),* and Dr. Linda Cripe, Professor of Pediatrics and Pediatric Cardiologist, reflect on Riley's journey.

Pat Furlong said, "This book is a group of stories about persistence, about changing medical attitudes, not accepting 'No.' It is about a family that can and will go to the ends of the earth... There are a number of stories in the midst of the Riley story."

Dr. Linda Cripe added, "The family handled it very well with a lot of grace and maturity, but at the same time, it's stressful. They were clearly 'all in,' and willing to do whatever it took to save their son. Willing to move to another state, which is a big deal. Some families aren't willing to do that."

Pat recalled, "The employer was also willing to allow that to happen. Both parents were working, and the employer could have said, 'You will lose your job.' Financial stability of the family then goes downhill because the care is intense. There are a lot of things that must go in favor of doing this transplant."

Linda chimed in, "It takes all the pieces to be 'all in' or you're not going to be successful if the medical community isn't willing to transplant."

"We've had families that say, 'You know we're not interested in heart transplant. We're going home. We're not willing to do this.' That happens probably 50% of the time."

"It's hard to get the consent of a 14-year-old kid who doesn't understand. I think in Riley's instance, he felt terrible. Sometimes when the kid is not feeling that bad, they might say, I'll just keep doing what I'm doing, I don't necessarily want my heart cut out."

Linda goes on to say, "It does take all those pieces to come together. It's sort of serendipity to make the magic happen. Like Pat said you must have the employer on board. You don't want the families to lose their jobs."

Pat responds, "There are many people on the waiting list. Everyone working together with the same belief for what's needed. People have become believers and are committed to make sure parents are given the best opportunity possible and employers are supportive for people to spend time with those they love. I think there's a lot of pain that happens along the way."

Linda comments, "From my perspective this is a different story because it was a historic problem that had not really been addressed in the United States. I don't think he was the first Duchenne boy who was transplanted. I think there may have been one or two prior to that. But being one of the first-- that was a gargantuan challenge. ...I think it's extraordinary, and Riley was an extraordinary patient."

Pat replies, "Love isn't enough! ... If you don't have a medical professional. If you don't have the people you're dealing with, on board with you. It's not enough. if you don't have the employer that is interested and willing. It's not enough, if you don't have support from other family members. It's not enough, that the policy stands as such a big obstacle because we don't transplant Duchenne's. Someone has to break that barrier for you."

"I think this *is* doing something that was impossible by really creating or changing minds of medical professionals and policies and making sure that all those barriers are taken down. It takes a village. Other hospitals refused to transplant Riley. It was serendipity. Love is not enough until you land on somebody who says, 'I'll try.'

Linda added, "It's really having all those pieces coming together in one place that helped to make this different."

Pat said, "It's about meeting up with the customer service representative who is following a policy that says, 'No.' Then, asking, 'Can I speak to your boss? If not your boss, another customer service representative?' Until you get to the point where someone says 'Yes.'"

Linda continues, "Taking ownership of Riley's healthcare was what drove his success. The parents were willing to be successful, but it was the advocacy organization [*PPMD*]. They turned to Pat and said, 'We need help. We can't get this done. What should we do?' The advocacy organization has those connections they've built in the community who are friendly to the Duchenne families or to that disease-specific family. So, then you can use those resources. It's sort of the secret sauce that I think more families need to know about. To know how to make the magic happen when you're having trouble getting it done."

Linda added, "It's about the perseverance and the partnerships."

"The texture of the story is not necessarily in Riley's singular story, but it's in the group of stories."

Pat reflects, "This is part of a big group of stories leading to success. I completely agree that this story needs to be told because I think it has far-reaching implications about what we do, how we make decisions, certainly who we give organs to, and under what circumstances. And how we sometimes change the medical community's perception when they feel a disease is hopeless."

Given the current landscape, I am uncertain if Riley would have received his heart transplant. It is of utmost importance for cardiologists worldwide to understand that just because boys with *Duchenne Muscular Dystrophy* (*DMD*) are often deemed terminal, it does not mean that their quality of life should be disregarded. Riley has been living with his new heart for 16 years, and I am optimistic that he has many more years ahead of him. Yet, he is still considered terminal to this day. Eat your words, all you disbelievers!

There's a saying that one person can make a difference; I believe that to be true. The one person for us was Pat Furlong.

A Mother's Love

Those we love don't go away;
They walk beside us every day.
Unseen, unheard but always near.
Still loved, still missed, and very dear.
Wishing us hope in the midst of sorrow, offering comfort in the midst of pain, both today and tomorrow.[32]

My mom has been a great influence on me throughout my life. Even in death, I find myself seeking her advice. Butte women are cut from a different cloth, capable of overcoming even the toughest circumstances.

189

When faced with rejection, they always find a way to persevere. It is not in the nature of Buttians to give up easily. They exhibit unwavering loyalty, especially when it comes to protecting their children, demonstrating a fierce and passionate maternal instinct.

Even today, at 54 years old, people will ask me where I'm from, and I will tell them Butte. Some will reply with a crass response, "OH, I'm sorry." I tell them, "I'm not!!" I'll give them every reason why I love Butte and defend it until the end. Butte has made me the person I am today, and I thank the good Lord above that I grew up there.

My mother was a trailblazer during her era, fearlessly delving into understanding *SMA* despite limited resources. If she were alive today, she might feel uneasy about the attention I am giving her in this book. As a private individual, she typically kept her personal affairs to herself. She often expressed her immense pride in Ron and me and our achievements with Riley. When I started writing this book, she was pleased, hoping it would raise awareness and foster understanding of *DMD*. Even if this book could save ONE life like Riley's, she believed sharing our family's journey would be worthwhile. My mother's whole goal was to make sure that we were all safe and happy, and she knew that I was doing that with Riley and Lexi.

Some days can be incredibly difficult, and simply making it through the day can feel like an impossible task. I miss my mom deeply every single day. The comforting thought of her presence used to bring me peace and a sense of calm. Knowing that there was someone who truly understood me as both a mother and a daughter made all the difference. I relied on her unyielding support, especially during life's toughest moments.

As a parent, you should be willing to give your children the shirt off your back. My mom demonstrated this selfless act every day while we were growing up. I believe Ron and I have followed in her footsteps by doing the same for Riley and Lexi throughout their lives. Ron and I have strongly committed our lives to providing the same level of care. I was so grateful that my mom was able to provide that support for me until the very end. She was a shining example of what it means to be the best parent possible.

Looking Back

The three most significant men in Riley's life have been Ron, Greg, and Dave. They have profoundly influenced Riley, shaping his character and contributing to the remarkable man he has become. They have stood by him through thick and thin, remaining a formidable presence in his life.

I vividly recall my conversation with Greg and Dave when Riley was young. I expressed my concerns about his participation in extracurricular activities. Their invaluable advice was to encourage his interests and engage him in activities that would allow him to excel. They warned against letting him passively watch TV and waste his potential. I took their advice seriously, striving to keep him active and involved during his formative years.

I remember one Halloween when Riley was in 5th grade, marking the final year he would partake in trick-or-treating. Riley was starting to struggle with walking long distances, and he opened up to Greg and Dave about his challenge. Greg and Dave traveled from Great Falls to lend their support. Uncle Buddy took Riley and Lexi around the neighborhood on the back of his wheelchair. That Halloween turned out to be the most memorable one for Riley. It was a heartwarming experience that Riley and Lexi would forever cherish, solidifying the bond with their uncles. These enduring memories have woven themselves into the fabric of their lives, serving as a reminder of the love and support that surrounds them.

Ron was constantly brainstorming ways to keep us engaged in the *PPMD* community. He demonstrated his support by participating in a half marathon at Disney World organized by *PPMD* as a fundraiser. Despite never having run a half marathon before, Ron, who always maintained excellent physical fitness, believed he could accomplish it with some training. After several months of preparation, he traveled to Orlando and completed over 13 miles to raise funds for *PPMD*. Running alongside other parents and family members, Ron expressed how honored he felt to support our *DMD* boys.

Another time, Ron reached out to his cousin Ricky Franchi, who resided in California. Their close relationship prompted Ricky to join our fundraising efforts eagerly after learning about *PPMD*. As the *California Soccer League* owner in San Diego, Ricky decided to organize a soccer tournament to raise funds. The tournament attracted hundreds of teams and was a resounding success. Ron flew to San Diego to assist Ricky in coordinating the event, and the proceeds were donated to *PPMD*.

I believe Riley's longevity can be attributed to how we have approached sharing information about his disease. We have always been mindful to provide details in small, age-appropriate doses, and he has never actively sought out more information. I believe this approach has contributed to his resilience and positive outlook on life. Riley has consistently defied the odds to the point where conventional expectations no longer seem to apply to him. He refuses to be defined by his heart transplant or his *DMD*; instead, he is defined by his character.

Riley has always possessed a strong sense of self, determination, and passion. He was surrounded by supportive friends and family who strived to normalize his life, and he has been uplifted and empowered throughout his journey.

We have raised Riley to be a warrior, and he has emerged as a beacon of resilience in the face of his condition. By surpassing perceived limitations and achieving the seemingly impossible, he stands as a testament to his strength. The transplant was a monumental peak in his climb, a testament to his survival and perseverance.

Our approach to life, shaped by Riley's perspective, mirrors the analogy of a Tootsie Pop. Rather than endlessly licking away at the surface, we have chosen to take a bite, savoring each moment's sweetness. Embracing this mindset has allowed us to appreciate our time together and revel in the joy it brings.

Riley has shattered barriers and defied expectations, consistently living in the present moment. While we acknowledge the past and anticipate the future, we approach each day with a sense of mindfulness and gratitude. Despite the physical toll that his condition takes, Riley remains steadfast in his resolve, managing the challenges with grace and care.

In the face of uncertainty, Riley persists in taming the metaphorical "Beast" that lurks in the background, maintaining a delicate balance through attentive care. While the journey ahead may hold challenges, we approach it with unity and determination, standing alongside Riley as he continues to inspire us with his unbelievable spirit.

If we had listened to every negative thing said about *DMD*, it would have destroyed us. Instead, we chose to forge our own path and shape our lives according to Riley's terms. We embraced the importance of living in the present moment and surrounded ourselves with knowledgeable and understanding individuals.

As we explore the complexities of living and aging with this disease, we embrace each day as it comes. Riley continues to hold onto his dreams and aspirations and looks forward to the future, not dwelling in the past. Our parenting philosophy prioritizes his comfort and well-being, ensuring that decisions are made collaboratively, with his input valued at every step. Riley will continue to live with us for the rest of his life because that is just the nature of "The Beast".

Nina & Ron

The definition of coincidence is a remarkable concurrence of events or circumstances without apparent causal connection. For example, they met by coincidence. I don't believe in coincidence. Ron and I met because fate brought us together. I was flabbergasted when we were first told that Riley's *DMD* and Greg and Dave's *SMA* were coincidental. I didn't believe it and still don't believe it today. The guilt of carrying that and thinking they are connected still keeps me awake at night. Nothing can be just left to coincidence. There has to be some force behind the scenes pulling the strings. It wasn't just a coincidence that Ron and I met. It wasn't just a coincidence that we had Riley. It wasn't just a coincidence that we found Pat Furlong and *PPMD*.

I'm acutely aware now that if I had been alone, who knows how things would have turned out if I had raised Riley alone? I might not have undergone the heart transplant for Riley. I'm tough and could have managed it, but it would have been significantly more challenging. I also think it would have been hard on Ron, knowing he had a child but wasn't involved in every aspect of raising him. He didn't want to be a part-time dad. Both of us desired to be a complete family.

With hard work, love can develop over time, and having children strengthens that bond. We are both family-oriented, so we made the decision together. It demonstrates that you can make good things come out of a difficult situation. We had no clue what would unfold after Riley was born and that he would be diagnosed with *DMD*. But if we had never crossed paths, who knows what might have been! It feels like fate brought us together.

We would never have experienced all these wonderful moments with Riley and Lexi. I've realized that we were meant to raise Riley this way. Our purpose was to help save his life and provide him with the best childhood and family life alongside his sister, Lexi. This was the Master Plan.

Riley's birth breathed new life into Greg and Dave, making them smile again. His diagnosis of *DMD* strengthened their resolve and helped them push forward. In return, they made him smile and pushed him forward throughout his disease.

Maintaining faith has given me the opportunity to raise the two most incredible children in the world. Now that they are both adults, I still have the privilege and honor of caring for Riley and supporting Lexi whenever she needs it. Riley's incredible journey has allowed me to reflect deeply on myself and determine who I want to become. Ron and I essentially grew up alongside them, as we were very young when we had them. As I continue to mature, I aspire to be Riley's supporter, caregiver, friend (when he needs one), chauffeur, physical therapist, chef, tutor, and housekeeper, but most importantly, I want to be his mom. I believe I'm doing reasonably well, but there's still more work to do.

At times, the sacrifices you make, no matter how agonizing they may seem, are for the greater good; however, you must have the strength to move forward. Things happen for a reason, and it is truly surreal when they come together as beautifully as they did in our case.

You can't just wish for things to happen; you must take action to make them a reality. Most of the time, this is done with the assistance of many others who, at that moment, choose to support you. I believe it must be the right moment and circumstances, and then the universe comes into alignment.

As Andy Dufresne said in The Shawshank Redemption, "Get busy living or get busy dying!"[33] Riley chose to get busy living. He continues to be an amazing fighter and possesses a strong sense of self. I don't think he will ever give up, and he deserves commendation for that. He doesn't allow anyone to hinder his progress. If someone offers to help him, that's wonderful. He considers everything and uses it as the motivation to keep pushing forward all these years. Having something to look forward to and being passionate about it is beneficial for him.

Unfortunately, there will come a time when this journey will end. In recent years, traveling or staying in hotels has become increasingly challenging. It's crucial for us to gather with family and friends to watch games and keep his interests alive, ensuring he always has something to look forward to.

The *Out*

Sometimes, I feel like I've trapped Ron because we were so young. Based on the genetic counseling I received, I was told it would be alright to have kids since I did not carry the SMA gene. I thought we were okay. Then we had Riley, who was diagnosed with Duchenne Muscular Dystrophy (DMD). I never want Ron to think I tricked him into marrying me. Even after giving him an "out" option every year for the last 32 years, the guilt still feels fresh and raw. Sometimes, it's all-consuming, but Ron always reminds me that we are in this together.

I couldn't have chosen a better partner to share this journey with. I love you, Ron!

Many parents who have been through similar situations end up getting divorced. I was raised to believe that couples stay together and make it work. Ron and I shared equal responsibilities. Without that, our marriage could have ended in divorce or separation. Raising a child alone would have been incredibly difficult. We have kept our marriage together, not just for the kids but for ourselves. We needed to be united and lean on each other. Riley is "our" child, and that's how we were raised. Parents with children needing this kind of support must work together.

In many cases, mothers handle a lot of the day-to-day challenges and need someone to support them. Fathers sometimes get a bad reputation, but they are working hard, too. Without the support of both parents, many marriages struggle to survive.

Robert Munsch wrote a children's book called *Love You Forever*. In it, there's a passage that says, "I'll love you forever, I'll like you forever, As long as I'm living, my baby you'll be."[34]

Riley has taught us humility, sympathy, empathy, pride, courage, strength, understanding, and unconditional love for our children. We will always be indebted to him for allowing us to be his mom and dad. We wish people could see you as we see you— a survivor, a warrior, a force for good, and an example of how people should live their lives. You have always believed everything will turn out okay and have never taken anything for granted. You strive to live your best life every day.

We tried to maintain balance in life for Riley and Lexi. There were moments when Lexi felt neglected, and Riley felt overwhelmed with attention. She was incredibly brave through it all. To this day, I struggle to let her go. I feel like I'm always trying to make up for the little child I had to leave behind to save the other. I was in a dilemma and never thought I would emerge from that tunnel. My parents were my guiding light; they helped me traverse through the tunnel and find light at the end of the tunnel.

During Riley's life, there were many times when we felt despair, only to be lifted up and carried across the finish line. Whatever your faith may be, believe that a higher power is leading you in the right direction.

Triumph of Hope and Faith

Being such a young family that had to deal with this deadly disease steals a little bit of your innocence. It makes you tougher, and being so young gives you that fighting spirit to go headfirst and do whatever you can for your child. When I look back at all we accomplished at such a young age, I think, "How did we ever pull this off?" I know that if we were older, I don't know if it would've happened the way it did. We were so young and full of life and determination. We carried the weight of the world on our shoulders and acted like it was nothing. We were bright-eyed and bushy-tailed newcomers to the game of *DMD*, and we were going to win.

As you grow older, you become more cynical and look at things through different eyes. You tend to find more excuses not to push as hard as we did. If we were to do it now, we would probably pull back the reins a little bit. That's why I am so incredibly grateful that we were able to pull off what we did at such a young age.

We have come to understand that, as parents, we are responsible for shielding our children from negativity and ensuring they are surrounded by positivity. In some parts of Peru, residents keep Guinea Pigs in their homes to absorb negative energies and bad karma. Similarly, as parents, we absorb any bad news or challenges that come our way, allowing Riley to lead a happy and fulfilling life.

Our parents would undoubtedly be proud of the family we have built today. I can picture them looking down on us with immense pride. Ron's parents would be especially pleased to see the loving father and provider he has become to Riley and Lexi and the support and love he shows me.

Riley embodies resilience and determination. The words "No" and "Can't" do not exist in his vocabulary. He always finds a way to overcome obstacles and challenges.

A true hero accepts praise and ensures their support system is acknowledged and appreciated. Pat Furlong epitomizes this quality, and Riley shares this trait. Despite being hailed as a hero by many, Riley humbly attributes his success to the incredible support system surrounding him.

Rules to Live By

We learned to focus on the positives and not dwell on the negatives. We discarded the old *DMD* handbook and created our own with the help of the *PPMD* community. Initially, when faced with the diagnosis, we armed ourselves with a wealth of information about the disease and potential complications. Much of the information we found online was alarming.

197

However, over time, we realized that many of the things we read did not pertain to Riley. Immersing ourselves in such negative information was disheartening and began to impact how we cared for him. We made a conscious decision to take our cues from Riley. Instead of letting "The Beast" define us, we define it.

Ron and I have gleaned valuable lessons throughout our journey of raising Riley.

Here are our rules for raising Riley with *DMD*:

1   *Parent Project Muscular Dystrophy (PPMD)* – When your child is first diagnosed, this is the most important phone call you will ever make. It will change you and your child's life forever!

2   Plan – Some boys develop *obsessive-compulsive disorder (OCD)*, and if things aren't explained in advance and planned early on, this can upset their routine.

3   Take things one step at a time -- Slow is Better. Don't always be in a hurry.

4   Get a good *Individualized Educational Plan* (*IEP*) started when they first enter school and keep it all the way through college.

5   Find something they're passionate about and foster that passion. For Riley, that passion is and has always been sports.

6   A word of caution: knowledge is power, but only in small doses.

7   Normalcy, normalcy, normalcy! (Thanks Mom!)

8   Prayer/having faith and hope.

9   Surround yourself with people who care about your son.

10 Patience is a virtue. Learning to have patience is vital if you want your child to be able to succeed. Even though it might take a few more tries and longer than expected, the accomplishment of completing the task is worth its weight in GOLD.

11 Self-Care: I cannot stress this enough. If you take care of yourself, you are better able to take care of your child.

12 Be Adventurous: Even though you're afraid your child will get hurt, let them try. You would be surprised at how well they

know their own limits. If Riley had never tried, he wouldn't have ridden a bike, driven a car, gone to college, etc.

13 Have a sense of humor: Laughter is the best medicine. Sometimes, if you don't laugh, you're going to cry. Laughing is so much healthier ☺

I know it might seem like a lot of rules, but *DMD* is a complicated disease. Trying to do it all alone can be lonely and dark. If you get lost, your son will get lost. Don't ever try to go it alone. *PPMD* will always be there; all you have to do is reach out. Don't give up, and your child is worth fighting for!!

Different Perspective

Sometimes, I ponder the journey we have all traveled. What if circumstances had been different? What if Riley had not been diagnosed with *DMD*? How different would our lives be today?

Many people often say, "God doesn't give you anything you can't handle." I'm not entirely sure if I believe in that notion. However, I believe and have witnessed that under extraordinary circumstances, people can accomplish extraordinary feats they never thought possible.

Riley reflects, "Many others have it worse than I do. My situation could have been far more challenging. I could have faced mental health issues, been confined to a wheelchair much earlier, or even lost my life due to not receiving a transplant. I am grateful for my parents' presence in my life. Thank you for being my mom and dad because I might not be here if circumstances were different."

Ron said, "I am blessed and honored to be his dad. I am blessed to have been able to do this for him. This isn't a cross I must bear. That makes it sound like I'm being forced into something I don't want to do, and I'm suffering. We don't live like that. That's not how we see things. It's as if something is heavy on your shoulders, and you can't lift it, and you can't reach your goal, but you keep trying, nevertheless. I've always looked at it as a parent. In my eyes, I can do anything and everything to be sure he has a good life. People tend to think they are weaker than they really are. They just haven't had to deal with something as major as *DMD*. There are many other people who deal with far more. I think about their struggle, and it makes me grateful. I'm not sad, disappointed, or upset. There is frustration, but you will always be frustrated with something this serious."

In terms of advice, "Ron and I firmly believe that we are here for a purpose, and we have navigated this journey to the best of our abilities. Human beings possess a remarkable resilience and strength that is often underestimated. When someone tells me, 'I don't think I could endure what you have,' my response is, 'Yes, you could. You have not yet been placed in a situation where you must confront your deepest fears, contemplate life and mortality, or face the mortality of your child. Your journey may have been smoother thus far, and that's okay. It's simply the luck of the draw. Embrace it, shape it according to your understanding, and redefine your life. Create a bright future for yourself and your children out of love, becoming their steadfast protector. They rely on you as their rock. It's essential to embrace the challenges presented to you. Some individuals may shy away from accepting these challenges because they doubt their own strength. However, they are capable and can rise to the occasion.' This is the beauty of the human spirit."

You must come to terms with how you choose to confront these challenges and remind yourself, 'This must be done, just for today, and then we move forward.' Take each day as it comes, one step at a time. Today is our present, and tomorrow is our future. The past holds significance only in reflection, such as in writing this narrative. Questions may arise, such as: Have I done everything in my power? What have I overlooked? Could I have acted sooner? Unexpected developments may stir feelings of dismay. Even when we believe we have everything under control, the challenges persist. This journey has no winners or losers; we simply exist in the 'now,' situated between victory and defeat.

We titled this book *The Life of Riley, Through a Mother's Eyes.* While our lives may have encountered more obstacles and challenges than many others, it does not diminish the goodness of our existence, the joy of our children's upbringing, or our unwavering efforts on their behalf. We have given our all, and I believe our best has been sufficient. *The Life of Riley* continues; our story is far from over.

Our determination to press forward stems from never dwelling on the past. Instead, our focus remains on the road ahead, steering clear of the rearview mirror. We have consistently reached our destinations, always affirming, "It is what it is."

In conclusion, Take what you've learned from the past. Focus on what you need to do, what your master plan is, and what you hope to achieve.

Riley's journey is an emotional one. I am retelling his story through my eyes. I want the reader to feel an emotional attachment because I think our emotions play a big part in who we are and how we're going to get things done.

You may be required to look deep within yourself and ask, "Am I capable of this? How far can I push myself?" This journey truly tests one's emotional resilience, as it presents significant challenges. Embracing the emotional aspect is crucial, given the difficulties ahead. Anticipating what lies in store for your child from a medical standpoint can be daunting. However, envisioning a future where your child surpasses those expectations and excels in school, drives, graduates, and secures a job requires determination and emotional strength.

Nina's Dad & Mom

Drawing from the experiences of my two brothers, I possessed the necessary background knowledge to chart our course and progress forward. Ron's intellectual prowess fueled his determination to research and control the path ahead. Utilizing resources like *PPMD* proved invaluable in this journey.

Ultimately, the decision rests on affirming, "We can do this." Harnessing one's intellect, understanding the necessary steps, and processing all information are vital components for achieving success. Cultivating hope and faith is equally essential.

My aspiration is for Riley's story to resonate deeply with others. Ron and I stand united in making informed choices, recognizing our collaborative efforts have been instrumental in our journey. As Ron aptly put it, "It's fate." Riley's miraculous heart transplant marked a pivotal moment where our decisions proved to be the right ones, benefiting Riley, Lexi, and ourselves. Thirty-one years later, we are still moving forward, guided by the conviction that we are making the right choices.

Life is fragile. We, as parents, are the caretakers of our children. Sometimes, tragedy can make you question your role as a parent, a friend, a relative, an aunt, or an uncle. To me, being a parent is a privilege that shouldn't be taken lightly. People sometimes take it for granted. Our time here on earth is so short.

Riley and Lexi are two of the bravest people I have ever met. Riley exemplifies bravery through his fighting spirit and steadfast determination to survive, while Lexi displays courage by entrusting Ron and me to help save her older brother.

I think as a parent who has raised a child with *Duchenne* to adulthood, we always just lived, taking it one day at a time. Parents tend to look ahead and at a lot of information about what their child's life will become. We have tried not to look at what's ahead because every child is different. Doctors told us, "There are things you can do for your child's health. Each child is different, and it's essential to live in the present and never look too far ahead." I think that's good advice that we have tried to follow.

I still wake up every day, hoping that it won't be his last. It's a terrible feeling to have, but one that I know parents with a child with DMD experience.

Every day is a gift from GOD!

Our life was extraordinary in an extraordinary way. For all the barriers and bumps in the road you deal with, don't let "The Beast" beat you down.

Day by Day

Our perpetual goal has always been and will continue to be keeping him alive today so he can live for tomorrow. Looking back, I had been preparing for this pivotal role my entire life.

Riley may claim he's not special, but it is precisely this humility that makes him exceptional. He is an extraordinary individual who wakes up each morning grateful for the gift of life.

I did a few speaking engagements after the transplant, but Riley never wanted me to talk about him and his or our experience. It was too personal for him. He wears his heart on his sleeve. I stopped and just focused on taking care of him and our family and getting him through high school, college, and dealing with all the other day-to-day things you have with a child who has *DMD*.

We have learned to embrace each day and be happy with life's small moments. So, if you find yourself with a spare moment after reading this book, remember that it can be challenging to always be on the inside looking out. Feel free to give us a call and drop by for a visit. We always make time for our family and friends. This book serves as a testament that Riley is still here and isn't going anywhere.

Recently, a doctor expressed surprise at Riley's well-being with *Duchenne Muscular Dystrophy* (*DMD*) and mentioned that he would be lucky if he lived past 50. Unfortunately, negative attitudes like these are not uncommon in the medical field. We quickly sought out another doctor who shared a more optimistic outlook.

We have often heard the phrase, "You are lucky to be alive!" However, luck has played no part in Riley's journey. Such statements contribute to the challenges faced by boys with *DMD* who are frequently overlooked for heart transplants. We were fortunate to have Pat Furlong and a remarkable team of doctors who saw beyond Riley's condition and recognized the potential benefits of a heart transplant for him. They took a chance and performed the transplant, but Pat Furlong SAVED HIS LIFE! We need to level the playing field when it comes to quality-of-life issues in transplanting a boy with *DMD*.

Riley has continued to fight "The Beast" for the past 31 years, with a bonus of 16+ years because of the heart transplant. Staying alive means everything to Riley and all those people who love him. That's why we fought so hard to keep him going all these years. Every day Riley wakes up is a miracle, a gift from God.

We could all learn a lesson or two from him. As Riley has poignantly said, "Living with *Duchenne Muscular Dystrophy* is better than being dead!" Spoken like a true survivor.

Duchenne Muscular Dystrophy (DMD): Research Now?

At present, *SMA* can be diagnosed with a simple blood test, while *DMD* still looks at *CPK* levels and genetic testing.

Even today, we encounter doctors who question Riley's diagnosis. They suggest that he may have *Becker* instead of *DMD*, stating that he wouldn't be alive if he had *DMD*. In response, Ron and I firmly assert that Riley does indeed have *DMD*. After all, his diagnosis was made by none other than Eric Hoffman, the renowned scientist who discovered the *Duchenne gene*. There is no doubt in our minds about the accuracy of Riley's diagnosis. What we need now is appropriate treatment and care.

Remember: There is hope! There is always Hope!

Chapter 8: Until We Meet Again

On November 23, 2023, God took Riley by the hand and led him into the arms of his loving Nanny, Papa, Omi, and Grandpa Gus. I had finished writing this book one week before he passed away. Now, through many tears, I write the final chapter.

Riley has always had a knack for surprising us when we least expect it. Just when everything seems to be going smoothly, he manages to catch us off guard with a bombshell. It leaves us with a profound sense of emptiness, unsure how to move forward. This was one bombshell that blindsided us completely. It has left a gaping hole we don't know how to fill.

My mother and I often discussed Riley, Dave, and Greg, sharing our fears and hopes for our sons. I vividly recall a specific conversation where we broached the topic of death. My mother confided that her greatest fear would be to outlive her sons. At that moment, I wholeheartedly shared her sentiment.

When your child dies, they don't just die once; they die every time you wake up and open your eyes. The pain of that empty space in your heart is indescribable, leaving you at a loss for how to mend the void. Perhaps, with time, healing will come.

If it weren't for Pat Furlong and her steadfast belief that Riley deserved a heart, he would have become another victim of *DMD* at the ripe old age of 14. Thanks to her, we were blessed with an additional 16 years to cherish and spend with this magnificent individual.

The night before he passed, Ron and I lay in bed beside him, each holding his hand. I remember him telling us. "I know you did the best you could. Thank you for everything you've done for me. I love you!"

Ecclesiastes III

To everything there is a season,
and a time to every purpose under the heaven:
A time to be born, a time to die;
A time to plant, and a time to pluck up that which is planted;
A time to kill, and a time to heal;

A time to break down, and a time to build up;
A time to weep, and a time to laugh;
A time to mourn, and a time to dance;
A time to cast away stones, and a time to gather stones together;
A time to embrace, and a time to refrain from embracing;
A time to get, and a time to lose;
A time to keep, and a time to cast away;
A time to rend, and a time to sew;
A time to keep silence, and a time to speak;
A time to love, and a time to hate;
A time of war, and a time of peace.[35]

The only way I can explain my grief of losing Riley is that it feels like death by 1000 paper cuts. The pain is incomprehensible. We would have done anything to keep him alive. We were willing to move heaven and earth. Now that I look back, I think that's exactly what we did, with a little help from Pat.

Dave and Greg often recount the tale of how, when Riley was around eight years old, he used to spend weekends with them in Great Falls. Riley's passion for sports was unparalleled, with a particular fondness for football. His greatest desire was to pursue a career playing his beloved sport. Regrettably, this aspiration was shattered by the cruel reality of becoming a helpless victim of the beast that is *Duchenne muscular dystrophy* (*DMD*).

One weekend, Dave went to the store and bought a Nerf football. They then took Riley to the park to play catch. I can imagine how happy Riley was at that moment, being able to play catch with the two uncles he loved so much. If I close my eyes, I can picture Riley going out for a pass and Uncle Buddy throwing him the ball, saying, "Go long!" I hope you are no longer in pain and are playing catch in heaven.

I was browsing through Riley's phone the other day and discovered he had a Holy Bible App. When I clicked on it, there was a verse of the day; it was 1 Corinthians 13:13. And now these three remain: faith, hope, and love. But the greatest of these is love.

Riley was always an optimist and believed in the afterlife. He had faith that we would do everything in our power to keep him alive, and his belief was unwavering. He had hope that we would find him a heart, and we did; it was a glimmer of light in the darkness. Riley knew that we loved him above all else and that love would endure beyond his passing. I often pondered what Riley truly needed, and I realized it was faith, hope, and love, the pillars that supported him through his journey. In the end, we managed to provide these essential elements. He held onto hope that one day, a cure for *DMD* would be discovered, putting an end to the suffering. While he was a realist and understood that a cure may have come too late for him, he held onto the possibility that it could halt the progression of the disease.

"The Beast" still lives on, but that doesn't mean he's won the war. Riley may have been defeated in his battle, but the war still rages on, and the lives of thousands of boys with *DMD* are at stake. More still needs to be done. Riley's quality of life mattered to Pat Furlong and her team at *CCH* and *PPMD*. They granted him an additional 16 years, and I want Riley's story to carry significance. His tale lives on through all those who have crossed paths with him. This book will uphold Riley's legacy, and I hope it will resonate with many more individuals, influencing how they perceive and treat boys with *Duchenne Muscular Dystrophy (DMD)*.

In Memory of Riley Herrera, age 31, of Helena, MT
April 11, 1992 – November 23, 2023

Riley Gustavo Herrera passed away Thursday, November 23, 2023, in Helena Mt. He was born on April 11, 1992, in Helena to Ron and Nina Herrera. Riley was born with *Duchenne Muscular Dystrophy (DMD)*. He gave it his all, but in the end, he succumbed to the all too familiar problems associated with *DMD*. He died at home surrounded by his loving family.[36]

Riley was a true warrior who battled his whole life with grace and humility. Riley never let this disease define him; on the contrary, he lived life on his own terms. So much so, that on March 31, 2007, he received a heart transplant at just 14 years old that would give him an extra 16 years to spend on this planet with his loved ones.

Riley surpassed all expectations of what he was told he could never do. He rode a bike, got a driver's license, graduated high school from Capital High and went on to graduate from Nevada State with a BA in Criminal Justice and a Minor in Psychology.

Riley was a sports fanatic who loved to watch his favorite teams on T.V. and in person. He was a beloved Griz fan. Go GRIZ! His other favorite teams included the Miami Dolphins, Gonzaga Bulldogs, USC Trojans and L.A. Lakers.

One of Riley's favorite things to do with his dad was hunting and fishing.

Riley loved driving his car to Great Falls, where he spent many weekends hanging out with his Uncles, Greg and Dave. He also loved spending time at the family cabin on Canyon Ferry Lake. He loved traveling, especially to exotic places such as Peru, Mexico, and the Bahamas.

Riley is preceded in death by his grandparents, Mary and Howard Stuart, and Inge and Gus Herrera. He is survived by his parents, Nina and Ron Herrera, his sister Lexi (fiancé Nick Wyman), and his loyal dog, Chico. Also included are his uncles, Greg, Dave, and Chris (Mahasin) Stuart. Rick, Dan (Chandra) and Steve Herrera. Aunts, Maria Tromly, Lisa (Jeff) Blanford. There were numerous cousins: Robert, Hayatee, Jazira, Aziz, Stefanie, Danielle, Kallie, and Laureli.

Friends are asked to join the family at Anderson Stevenson Wilke Funeral Home on Monday, November 27, 2023, from 1-3 PM to celebrate his life.

Private interment of ashes will take place at a later date.

Donations in memory of Riley can be made to *Parent Project Muscular Dystrophy* (*PPMD*) at https://www.parentprojectmd.org/.[37]

I know that losing a child is the most horrific and heartbreaking experience anyone can endure. In my own journey with Riley and his battle with *DMD*, I came to terms with the fact that his disease was incurable and would eventually claim his life—it was just a matter of time.   As I reflect on Riley and all the parents struggling with their boys, I advise showering them with as much love as you can AND making sure to be their strongest advocate. **YOU** are singularly the best chance at their survival. Maintain your faith, cling to hope, and provide them with the best care in a loving and nurturing environment.

Ultimately, in the end, "the beast" that is *Duchenne Muscular Dystrophy* took our beautiful, beloved son, but it wasn't without a fierce fight! Keep on fighting!!

Our grief is suffocating and devastating, but during the dark hours, I can hear Riley's voice saying to me, "Some people have it worse."

Having Riley as my son for the last 31 years has been an absolute honor and a blessing.

To Riley, "This isn't goodbye; It's until we meet again. I love you, my dear son!!!"

Reflecting on our journey, I wouldn't change a single thing. I wholeheartedly believe that every experience has led us to this point, and altering our path would have meant missing out on the joy of having Riley in our lives. It was meant to be!

Remember: There is hope! There is always Hope!

References

1 Duchenne Muscular Dystrophy (DMD). Retrieved on July 2, 2022, https://www.mda.org/disease/Duchenne -muscular-dystrophy

2 Zig Ziglar. Retrieved on July 7, 2023, https://medium.com/@kristarausin/f-e-a-r-has-two-meanings-forget-everything-and-run-or-face-everything-and-rise-bb5c8dd676fc.

3 Hoffman, Eric. Faculty and Staff, Binghampton University, State University of New York. Retrieved on July 21, 2023, at https://www.binghamton.edu/pharmacy-and-pharmaceutical-sciences/about/profile.html?id=ehoffman.

4 Hoffman, Dr. Eric. (1996) Recreation of hand-drawn chart provided to parents.

5 Chaytow H., Faller K.M.E., Huang Y.-T., Gillingwater T.H. Spinal Muscular Atrophy: From Approved Therapies to Future Therapeutic Targets for Personalized Medicine. Cell Rep. Med. 2021;2:100346. Retrieved on March 26, 2024 at https://www.ncbi.nlm.nih.gov/pmc/articles/PMC10418635/#:~:text=In%20199 5%2C%20two%20SMA%2Drelated,in%20the%20US%20%5B15%5D.

6 Rae, Mark G. and O'Malley, Dervia. (2016). Cognitive dysfunction in Duchenne muscular dystrophy: a possible role for neuromodulatory immune molecules. American Physiological Society. Retrieved March 23, 2024 from https://www.ncbi.nlm.nih.gov/pmc/articles/PMC5023417/#:~:text=However% 2C%20dystrophin%20is%20also%20expressed,%2Dterm%2C%20and%20wo rking%20memory.

7 Joncas, Michael. (1989). On Eagles Wings. Retrieved on March 22, 2024 at https://genius.com/Michael-crawford-on-eagles-wings-lyrics.

8 Cast, Kristi. (June 3, 2021) Quotes of Famous People, Betrayed. Retrieved on June 7, 2023, at https://quotepark.com/quotes/1379799-kristin-cast-ignorance-breeds-fear-and-hatred/.

9 March of Dimes Peristats. (Updated January 2022) retrieved on May 21, 2023, https://www.marchofdimes.org/peristats/data?reg=99&top=14&stop=131&sle v=4&obj=3&sreg=30.

10 Duchenne Muscular Dystrophy (DMD). Retrieved on July 2, 2022, https://www.mda.org/disease/Duchenne -muscular-dystrophy

11 Chalker, Brian A., "Drew." (2021) Aesthetic Poems. Retrieved on June 7, 2023, https://aestheticpoems.com/reason-season-lifetime-poem/.

12 Gray, John. (1992) Men Are from Mars, Women Are from Venus. retrieved on March 29, 2024, at https://en.wikipedia.org/wiki/Men_Are_from_Mars,_Women_Are_from_Venus

13 Herring, Nicole. (2024) Parent Project Muscular Dystrophy: President's Bio. Retrieved on March 19, 2024 at https://www.parentprojectmd.org/about-ppmd/staff-board/presidents-bio/

14 Ibid.

15 Bombeck, Erma. (March 12, 1971). If Life is a Bowl of Cherries, What Am I Doing in the Pits? Fawcett Books.

16 Milne, A. A. (Alan Alexander), 1882-1956. (2003). Winnie-the-Pooh. [New York], Harper Children's Audio.

17 Dickens, Charles. (1859). A Tale of Two Cities. Opening paragraph. Retrieved on January 12, 2024 at https://www.goodreads.com/work/quotes/2956372-a-tale-of-two cities#:~:text=It%20is%20a%20far%2C%20far,than%20I%20have%20ever%20known.

18 Lupica, Mike. (February 5, 2013) New York Daily News. Remembering Arthur Ashe The First African American to Win Wimbledon. Retrieved April 1, 2024, from https://www.nydailynews.com/2013/02/05/remembering-arthur-ashe-the-first-african-american-man-to-win-wimbledon-who-died-20-years-ago/

19 https://lostandfoundation.org

21 (March 22, 2007). Around The Town, Fundraisers, Lost and Foundation. Helenair Newspaper.

22 Powers, Margaret Fishback. (1964) Footprints Poem. Retrieved May 12, 2022, https://footprintssandpoem.com/margaret-fishback-powers-version-of-footprints-in-the-sand/

23 Welker, Maureen. (August 5, 2022) Psychosis Definition. Retrieved July 22, 2023, https://www.medicinenet.com/icu_psychosis/article.htm

24 https://www.mdpi.com

25 Guier, Cindy (March 9-15, 2008). Encouraging Coaches. American Profile, Northeast edition Sunday Magazine

26 Guier, Cindy (March 9-15, 2008). Encouraging Coaches. American Profile, Northeast edition Sunday Magazine

27 Ibid.

28 Ben Stein Quotes. (n.d.). BrainyQuote.com. Retrieved March 22, 2024, from BrainyQuote.com Web site: https://www.brainyquote.com/quotes/ben_stein_383479

29 King, Stephen, (1982). Shawshank Redemption. Retrieved August 12, 2023, https://online.visual-paradigm.com/flipbook-maker/templates/quotes/get-busy-living-or-get-busy-dying-stephen-king/#:~:text=Shawshank%20Redemption%3A%20A%20Story%20from,its%20importance%20to%20the%20story.

30 Spinks, Leon. (1953) Retrieved on June, 22, 2023 from https://www.brainyquote.com/quotes/leon_spinks_439144

31 Crawford, Roger. (March 24, 2020). Being Challenged in Life is Inevitable, Being Defeated is Optional. Retrieved on February, 22, 2024 from https://rogercrawford.com/product/challenges-are-inevitable/

32 Annonymous.

33 King, Stephen, (1982). Shawshank Redemption. Retrieved August 12, 2023, https://online.visual-paradigm.com/flipbook-maker/templates/quotes/get-busy-living-or-get-busy-dying-stephen-king/#:~:text=Shawshank%20Redemption%3A%20A%20Story%20from,its%20importance%20to%20the%20story.

34 Munsch, Robert. (1995). Love You Forever, Firefly Publisher.

35 The Bible King James Version. Ecclesiastics 3: 1-8. Retrieved January 3, 2023, from Versionhttps://www.bible.com/bible/1/ECC.3.1-8.KJV

36 Anderson Stevenson Wilke & Retz Funeral Home. (November 27, 2023). In Memory of Riley Herrera, Helena, Montana.

37 Ibid

www.ingramcontent.com/pod-product-compliance
Lightning Source LLC
Chambersburg PA
CBHW060022100426
42740CB00010B/1559